A NOVEL

ONE THOUSAND

One Thousand Porches

ISBN: 978-0-692-65256-5
Library of Congress Control Number:

Book design by Sabach Design
sabachdesign.com

Published & Distributed by
HOLLAND PRESS
7640 Edgecomb Drive
Liverpool, New York 13088

www.juliedewey.com
info@juliedewey.com

Publisher's Cataloging-In-Publication Data
(Prepared by The Donohue Group, Inc.)

Names: Dewey, Julie.
Title: One thousand porches : a novel / Julie Dewey.
Description: Liverpool, New York : Holland Press, [2016] | Previously
    published: [CreateSpace], [2013].
Identifiers: ISBN 978-0-692-65256-5
Subjects: LCSH: Physicians--Fiction. | Tuberculosis--Patients--Fiction. |
    Sanatoriums--New York (State)--Saranac Lake--Fiction. | Healing--
    Psychological aspects--Fiction. | Saranac Lake (N.Y.)--Fiction.
Classification: LCC PS3604.E949 O54 2016 | DDC 813/.6--dc23

Printed in the United States of America

DEDICATION

This book is dedicated to my great grandmother,
Lena Green Thompson.
While I did not know her personally,
I know she had strength, fortitude, and resilience,
for she was a woman who suffered from consumption
during a time when there was no cure.
She lived to be 96 years old.

CONTENTS

❧

PART
ONE

CHRISTINE
1885

CHAPTER 1

❧

PITTSBURG, NEW YORK 1885

The sputum most likely crossed the hearth of our large country estate in Pittsford, New York, on the scalloped hem of my favorite green velvet dress; the flattering ensemble with the well-fitted bodice and bustle below my waist in the back. I was told this by my husband, James Lyndon, who made me watch while he set the garment to burn in our charred grate, the embers coursing through the fabric, destroying the residue left from a lunger's hacking.

Consumption was a poor man's disease. It was inconceivable that it gained entry into our pristine home miles outside the village by any other means. James had no one else to hold responsible for his son's suffering, so in his eyes, the burden of blame was mine. I had ventured into town for our grocery staples and bolts of fabric on one occasion, and on another, I collected miniature pumpkins for the hearth and crimson mums for the porch. As always, I lunched with the ladies on the first and third Wednesday of the month. I dared not remind my husband, but he ventured far more places than I did, and far more often.

My husband could not bear witness as his son's flesh was consumed, his lungs gurgling and dissolving as he gasped and choked for air. All Henry's strength and will were sapped from his body as he withered away in isolation, his soul leaving us for heaven mere weeks before his eighteenth birthday celebration in October. I was given no choice but to accept the guilt that Henry would never attend college, or marry and have children of his own. James placed the blame squarely upon my shoulders and defiantly closed me out of our bedroom and his affections, punishing me for the death of our firstborn son.

Typically solid and stoic to a fault, James became maniacal for a short time immediately following Henry's death. He smashed the porch pumpkins with their carved smiling faces until there was nothing left of them but the pulp. Frenzied, he set off on a tirade where he emptied gown after gown from my closet, along with dress coats, shoes, scarves, and gloves, flinging them all into the raging blaze to be destroyed. James wasted no time storming through the house ripping sheets and pillowcases off beds, kitchen aprons from hooks, old fraying rags from under our sink, all set to burn.

"James, you cannot burn our entire wardrobes, we will have nothing left!" I screamed in a panic, trying to get through to him. But I knew I could not be heard, for his empty eyes did not meet mine. Instead, they flickered across the house, leaping from object to object in search of anything else he missed; telling me in short, he was momentarily insane.

Amidst my pain and suffering, I took great measures to prevent the bacteria from infecting the rest of us. I began with scouring the house daily on my hands and knees to an immaculate state until my fingers cracked and bled. In the evenings, my gentle and thoughtful daughters slathered my hands, one finger at a time, with petroleum jelly and wrapped them with strips of cotton placed in "v" shapes in order to heal. All of my remaining dressing gowns, the ones set aside to be tailored that James missed as he ransacked the place, as well as

Collette's and Emma Darling's, were hemmed to mid-calf so they did not risk contact with the ground. Lucas and Daniel, our two remaining boys, wore trousers that did not drag, but I feared the disease and their father's instability so intensely now that I made them take off their shoes on the porch and wipe the soles with rags dipped in boiling water the moment they got home from school. Then the rags were burned in our outdoor fire pit.

We were told the disease could lay dormant for months or years, causing even more panic. So the fires raged, and our old shifts were ripped to make rags for boiling and cleaning purposes.

The disease, known as consumption, white plague, the red death, or tuberculosis, was especially harmful to anyone with an already compromised immune system, such as our Collette, with her weakling lungs. It was spreading like wildfire across the nation and was being touted as the most fatal disease known to man, far surpassing typhoid and scarlet fever in its death toll. It took nearly one in every seven Americans or four hundred souls daily. It showed no prejudice in whom it afflicted either. The elderly as well as children, men, and women, black and white, poor and wealthy, were disposed of, but most often it was young adult males in the prime of their life, like our Henry, falling prey.

Doctors and scientists were perplexed by the spread of the disease; some believed it developed based on the patient's constitution, either physiologically or psychologically, and therefore didn't believe it could be spread. Along the same lines, other scientists and researchers believed it to be hereditary and therefore took no precautions against it. Still others thought it was airborne and spread from spitting, coughing, laughing, sneezing, and even talking. It was thought by these folks that it could also be transferred from bodily fluids, such as pus and bowel discharge. Doctors encouraged everything from wearing beards for men to prevent the germ from entering their orifices, to eating nothing but diets rich in meat and dairy.

"I tell you, Christine, this disease is contagious. We must be vigilant about our hand washing. Furthermore, wife, we shall each bathe nightly in separate water," James spoke to me through his fog of grief.

Although my husband had mostly been restored and calmed since his tirade weeks ago, his anguish was raw and he remained obsessive over our cleanliness and compulsive over where we went and with whom we spent our time.

"I don't wish to see anyone," I said one bitter cold evening in November before guests were due to arrive for the dinner hour. The guests were friends of Henry's coming to pay their respects, but I wished only to have my family around me now. Admittedly, I was also thinking ahead to the additional disinfecting having company would mean for me tomorrow, not to mention the fear James instilled in me with the contagious nature of the disease.

"Would you like me to send a cancellation notice?" my husband asked. He stood before me, pursing his lips, hands on his narrow hips, searching my eyes for an answer.

"That would be kind, perhaps send a parcel of flowers begging for forgiveness as well," I answered, as I snuggled deeper into the davenport rather enjoying the afghan around my shoulders, enveloping me in warmth.

Our days spent mourning Henry left us all with gaping holes in our hearts, and none of us were in the mood for entertaining guests where we would be forced to discuss trivial matters and play at cards halfheartedly. Or worse, summon Henry's image and open us to the suffering once more.

During this quiet time, Emma Darling practiced her scales on the piano and Collette and I paid closer attention to our embroidery and correspondence with family members who resided in Skaneateles. The boys tended to their studies and James filled any and all of his free time with meetings and work as an architect and freelance contractor for the Erie Canal. His designs took him far away from the pain, and us. He feared being in our home where the smell of death lingered in the corners. However, he did not feel vulnerable going to the supposedly germ-free homes of strangers or acquaintances to draft outlines.

"We are here, James, look at us, look at me! We are alive and you treat us as if we all died with Henry." I admonished my husband for his abandonment when I was at a weak moment one tranquil evening when he came home for a change of clothing. I begged him to take me back into his bed and hold me once more, gesturing with wide sweeping arms toward the library where the boys studied and the parlor where the girls practiced harmonies.

"Christine, never speak his name to me again," he instructed, and left me with his fingerprints across my smarting cheek. It was the first time he struck me, and it stunned me into silence. What had become of my husband of twenty years? James was always stable and kind and was never a man to raise his hand at a woman or child. He was soft spoken, had delicate features and a neatly trimmed beard, he was well known and enjoyed for his company around town. I took his warning and cried into my pillowcase in the guest bedroom that night, not wishing to startle the children. He refused to let me into his heart, and while I understood his pain, I was growing resentful.

Not being in the mood for company any longer, our once sizable staff was whittled down to one maid and one cook. Although we trusted them both, they were subject to a litany of questions regarding their health and were studied for any symptoms before we allowed them a shoe-less entry into our home. We kept clean slippers at the ready for our help, so no one had reason for complaint of cold feet during the dark, damp winter months.

If anyone in the household developed a sniffle or slight cough, they were immediately ordered into quarantine. Water and nutrition in all manner of forms, but most often soups and broths, were left by the door for the sick patients to fetch themselves. The rest of the household waited impatiently for other symptoms of plague to appear; chills and fever often accompanied a cough with an average cold or flu, but when the cough went from intermittent to constant, everyone worried.

So far, we had sustained our pace of keeping house and going about our usual practices, but with the holidays fast approaching we feared numerous gatherings and consequently bringing the harbinger of death back into our lives.

"Collette, Emma Darling, Lucas, Daniel, come here please, children." I ushered the children into the living room for a discussion.

"Coming, Mother," the girls chimed in unison before settling themselves, legs crossed, on the rich brown velvet davenport.

"I have spoken with your father and although he is not here this evening, he wants me to discuss the holidays with you. It will be our first Christmas without Henry. Your father and I would like to spend the days quietly at home this year rather than travel to Skaneateles to see your cousins."

"Mother, no! I want to write plays and dance with Celia and Marianne!" Collette protested.

"I know, Collette, perhaps in the spring we may pay them a visit." I addressed her with compassion, for I knew how much she enjoyed this special time with her cousins.

"But, Mother it will be so lonely here if it's just us, it won't seem like Christmas at all." Little Daniel spoke from his heart, in his eight years the holidays always meant time with extended family.

"We can make our own plays, children. Why, we can even make a puppet theater and make tiny furniture and costumes. If you'd like, we can decorate our own house this year and tell stories by the fire."

"Can we make popcorn garlands, Mother?" Emma Darling asked.

"Why, yes, we can, and we can make ornaments as well with navel oranges and cloves just as I did when I was your age. We can also make gingerbread cut-outs and tie them with string. It will be lovely." I could already picture the balsam pine in our living room decorated with these loving touches.

The reality was that James could hardly face the upcoming season. He filled his schedule so tightly we would have little time for travel regardless. Additionally, we didn't know what measures were taken in our relatives' home to prevent consumption, nor did we know how they felt having us as company, considering we could be harbingers. Skaneateles did not yet have strict rules for lungers and others suspected of being ill as our tiny town did. Our village was hit hard, losing hundreds of lives in the fall, so a board was formed and the village of Pittsford took great pains to prevent the disease from spreading. Spittoons were placed along each of the streets spreading out from the four corners Phoenix Hotel. Similarly, they were positioned in front of the many booming dining establishments that my husband designed and about which our town boasted. If ever a lunger spit in the spittoon, it was immediately flushed with boiling water. If someone suspicious hacked into a handkerchief or napkin, it was burned immediately by an errand boy.

The village board devised posters and led anti-spitting campaigns.

Rule number 1. Don't spit

Rule number 2. Do not let others spit.

Rule number 3. If you have a cough and must spit, do it in a napkin and burn it in a stove.

Rule number 4. Repeat rule number 1.

Posters were hung on establishment doors throughout our village, and nearly everyone complied. Everyone feared the incurable, deadly disease and most wouldn't wish the overwhelming suffering on their greatest enemy.

CHAPTER 2

⁂

SPRING, 1886

"It has been six months already, it hardly seems right," I said one evening to the girls while tucking them snuggly in their twin beds. I gathered their toes in the cushioning warmth of their matching comforters just as they liked.

"Mommy? What do you suppose heaven is like?" Emma Darling, with her always inquisitive mind, asked.

"I don't know for sure, but I imagine it's very peaceful and happy. Like a meadow on a perfect sunshiny day with a soft breeze and the sweet smell of lilacs and primroses in the air. Birds are chattering and my children are playing and laughing. I can only hope, Little Dove, that this is what my heaven shall be like!"

"I wonder what Henry's heaven is like, do you think it has lots and lots of books for him to read?" she chattered on.

"I am sure of it!" I answered, for Henry had been the most studious of all my children and was rarely seen without a book. Collette was silent during our exchange; when I attempted to bring her in to our conversation, she swiftly turned her head, not wanting to discuss heaven in all its glory. It had consumed her brother and that hardly made her happy.

Collette, who was fifteen, and Emma, who was ten, shared a room and said their prayers side by side nightly, always including their beloved Henry in their thoughts. Lucas, who was swiftly approaching fifteen, and Daniel, my baby at eight, also shared a room. Fatefully, only Henry had slept alone, keeping the plague from spreading.

Time stretched on and the children and I began to heal through the anonymous gifts of spring. A bunny skittering across the wild dandelion-infested lawn, the season's first robin scampering about building its nest with last year's grasses, the effortless grace of the daffodils' fragrant bloom, all these vestiges of life renewed our spirits.

The gray winter swept behind us now, we heaved open our windows and beckoned the warm spring breeze indoors to tickle our skin, giving us goosebumps. Everyone, myself included, felt a false sense of security given the seasonal change. Coughs dissolved, people followed the rules for spitting, and few cases of tuberculosis were reported.

"Children, how about a picnic along the canal today?" I asked on a particularly lovely day.

"Oh yes, Mommy, can we ride our new bicycles and bring our fishing poles, too?" Daniel asked.

"I don't see why not," I answered, and a flutter of activity began as the girls and I packed sandwiches and apples for lunch, while the boys dug into the damp earth in search of plump worms they could use for fish bait.

James had purchased the boys their very own "high wheel bicycles" from a new merchant in town at Christmastime. The merchant told them to select a rubber wheel as long as their legs would allow. The merchant explained that the larger the wheel the further the boys would travel with just one rotation of the pedal. They were anxious to go for a ride and couldn't wait to fish along the Erie Canal. They had fishing poles ready, and Lucas carried bait in a pail. Daniel carried the lunches I packed.

The girls and I desired new bolts of fabric for fresh dresses and bonnets. We strolled, arms linked, through town feeling the buoyancy of spring. We stopped in to bid good day to friendly merchants, and found everyone in town to be as cheerful as we were. We took great pains when selecting fabrics for our new dresses, running our fingers across the lush blue and plum-colored velvets and the rich jewel-toned silky satins. The new bold calico and print selections were terribly tempting as well. After perusing the pattern books and shelves stocked with hundreds of spools of lace and ribbon, alongside dozens of jars of buttons, we each had an idea of what our new attire would look like, bonnets included. We left the store with our purchases wrapped and tied into tidy parcels to meet up with the boys and enjoy a picnic along the canal.

It was such a pleasant day that I dare say Henry left my mind for a moment. I didn't fret or feel drowned in guilt; instead I enjoyed laying with my back pressed on the earth, allowing the mid-day sun to shine upon me and my children. After our picnic, we strolled along the canal for a bit. I was always conscious of Collette's lungs, knowing she couldn't walk for as long or as far as the rest of us and often needed to take a rest along the way. She would take a seat on a large rock along our pathway and the boys would prop their high wheels on their kickstands and take this time to skip rocks into the water, which had become a large part of our life. They sang as they skipped rocks and had a jolly time indeed.

The Erie Canal was constructed in order to provide reliable transportation for goods going West. It extended from Albany, New York, on the Hudson River to Buffalo, New York, at Lake Erie, creating a passable water route to the Atlantic Ocean and the Great Lakes. The canal transportation system was faster and more reliable than horse and buggy and was more cost effective than the railways. Pittsford's population and economic growth boomed during this time. The flour mill, Pittsford Farms Dairy, lumberyards, and produce warehouses all took advantage of the system that created great wealth and spurred on the suburban sprawl that took place. The building of numerous country estates was the first step in moving Pittsford from a farming community to a suburb. James was commissioned to design grand estates for railroad contractors and owners of the larger operations such as the flour mill. With so much new business in town, my husband was busy sketching all day and night for new homeowners. James rarely graced us with his presence any longer, but when he did, his fingers were stained with ink and the gaping hollows beneath his eyes told me he had not slept. I wondered if there was another woman but did not dare to ask. He claimed to be at his office in town, sleeping on the davenport and eating at the Brookwood Inn, his favorite restaurant.

When Collette began with a gentle cough, a tickle in her chest, it was several days before he knew. I isolated her in the guest room, far away from her siblings, and summoned our doctor, to whom I spoke of her mild symptoms. I told the doctor about our walk along the canal several days prior to her cough and because he already knew she had weak lungs he glared at me with disdain for allowing it. He wanted to administer a chloroform liniment directly to her chest to help with her bronchospasms, but I required the approval of James first.

"A liniment, what in the world is that?" James inquired when he stopped home for a change of clothing.

"It's a salve of sorts, a rubbing mixture that I will apply to her chest thrice daily to dull her pain and ease her coughing spasms."

"Oh no, you won't. You won't step foot through her doorway, Christine. What if it's consumption?" he glared at me critically.

"It's not consumption, James, I am sure of it. We have paid our dues. It is her weak lungs acting up from the walk I led her on a few days ago." I stared at the ground upon my admission, afraid to meet his eyes. When I looked up, I could see the steam coming out of his ears as he tried to remain composed, both of us afraid he would go insane once more. Surely he didn't expect me to allow the boys to go riding their high wheels alone and surely he understood our need to escape the dungeon our home had become in search of fresh air.

"She does not have weak lungs! That is all in her head, for crying out loud. Christ, woman, you could get us all infected and killed! Have you no mercy?" He was pacing as he spoke.

"Have I no mercy? How dare you? I am the only one in this marriage any longer, caring for the children alone. Mercy? You speak to me of mercy yet you forbade me from comforting Henry in his last days! That's mercy, husband, which you have none of!" I spun on my heels and stormed out of the parlor up into the hallway to listen to the sounds from Collette's room and calm myself from speaking to my husband so brazenly.

The calm did not come. My blood was boiling and I was seething. Mercy? How dare James speak to me of having mercy? He would rather listen to the suffering of his child than allow me entry to offer comfort. Collette was different from Henry; she was delicate and worrisome. She needed her mother and I would go to her no matter what. I tidied my hair into a tight bun, smoothed my skirt, and took up my latest cross-stitch on the porch, far away from my husband, assuming he would be gone momentarily. But he didn't leave this evening; instead, he sat smoking his pipe, with a faraway wistful look in his eye.

I approached him from behind and lay my hand upon his shoulder. We had been through challenging times before, and we could get through this too, if only he would let me in. "What do you want now, Christine?" he asked in a whisper.

"I want the liniment. I can't stand to stay idle while she suffers."

I kneeled at my husband's side and placed my hand softly on top of his. "Don't you remember her as a little girl? Collette always had a green nose and rattle in her chest, and I assure you this is nothing more."

I hoped for reassurance, but it was too much to ask. My husband of twenty years stood to take his leave. "Where will you sleep tonight?" I asked boldly, wondering if he would tell the truth, although I didn't want to hear it.

"At my office, where else do you think I've been?" he asked accusingly while he stroked his neatly trimmed brown beard.

"I suppose I have wondered once or twice if there were someone else, younger perhaps?" If he had another woman, I wanted to know now.

"No. There is no one else, Christine, it just pains me too much to be here. I know it's not fair to you or the children but my heart, it's just split and I can't bear it," he confessed.

"Husband, come to bed with me, please?" I begged, realizing that the emotional torture he suffered from was worse than my own. I had the children to comfort me and distract me; I had their loving arms about my waist and shoulders, and we shared countless tears as well as precious butterfly kisses. We reminisced over our beloved Henry, and it was healing. My husband had none of this, and in fact, the tenderness of another was precisely what he needed. I reached for his lapel and gazed into his dark blue eyes, his face grave and lonely.

It took coaxing, but at last he put out his pipe and climbed the stairs with me for the last time. I led him to our bed, expecting only to tuck him in and allow him a peaceful slumber. Surprisingly, he grabbed my hand and pulled me to him.

"Forgive me?" he asked.

"Always," I responded. The pain he caused me by accusing me of Henry's demise stemmed from his fear, so forgiving him was easy. Going back to bed with him took a bit longer. We were like young lovers, unsure how to behave, each one afraid of displeasing the other.

In the morning, the children were delighted by their father's presence and spoke over one another to get his much-needed attention. I hoped my prayers were answered and that he would become a part of our lives once more so that we could all heal together. However, I couldn't help the sinking feeling I had in my gut when I caught sight of Emma Darling.

"I will get the liniment from Doctor Hill this morning and have an errand boy bring it to you so you may begin applying it at once." He kissed me on my forehead and left with a kick in his step and hot buttered toast in his hand. James had not noticed the violet circles beneath Emma's eyes and the leaden way she moved, as if her body was thrice her weight. Her eyes were bright and cheeks flushed a rosy hue. I put my palm across her forehead, and she felt warm. I had no time to catch James and tell him the news, he was already off to meet with clients about the latest drafts he had drawn up for their home. The boys were sent outdoors and Emma Darling was put straight away to bed, the door shut behind her.

When the errand boy came with the liniment for Collette, I sent him with a note back to James.

> *Dear James,*
>
> *I beg of you to forgive me. Emma Darling has come down with a cough and her demeanor frightens me. Perhaps it is best if you take the boys this evening, I have ushered them outdoors since you left this morning. I fear the worst.*
>
> *Your Loving Wife, Christine*

Emma Darling spent the following two weeks in her bedroom. My daughter was positioned by the window so she could take in as much sunlight as possible as per the doctor's orders. Her room was to be airtight and she was to be cocooned at all times, which she abhorred. She began with a fierce but intermittent cough, then the hacking became more constant and filled her lungs with yellow and green phlegm tinged with blood. The doctor spoke with me on the porch as I rattled off Emma's symptoms. He felt certain she was suffering from consumption but agreed to examine her after seeing Collette. Emma coughed as the doctor listened to her lungs and just as he anticipated, her right lung was afflicted with active tuberculosis disease.

"It hurts, Mother," she said, after the doctor left, "like a hot stoker sitting on my chest whenever I cough." Her lips were chalky and white, and her skin a gray pallor.

"I know, my darling girl, I have spoken with the doctor, and I am certain that he has a liniment we can use for you." I was less than hopeful but tried disguising my voice when it cracked. I watched my daughter struggle with each breath. Her fingernails were pale like her skin so I knew she was not circulating air properly. Her eyes were glassy and red-rimmed, just like Henry's.

"Not my Emma Darling, please, God. I beg of you to take me, not my daughter. I can't lose another child to this horrendous disease. Please be gentle with her, help her to breathe and help all of us get through this," I prayed fervently day in and day out.

Collette was doing far better and was now allowed from her room. Her cough was indeed induced by asthma as I suspected and the mentholated liniment helped break up the bronchospasms that plagued her.

The liniment tincture did not have the same effect on poor Emma and the doctor felt she was rapidly deteriorating. She was deathly pale and very weak, the wracking coughs leaving her with little to no energy. I turned her sideways and cupped my hands, then pounded her back up and down her left side first from shoulder to waist, and then up and down her right side from shoulder to waist. I repeated this procedure to relieve the lungs of the mucus, and draped warm cloths across her chest to loosen her muscles and help temper the pain. She coughed up so much sputum the bucket at her bedside grew rank. I emptied it, then sloshed it with boiling water, sloshing and scrubbing my hands and fingernails thoroughly as well.

James was inconsolable. We only spoke through letters now; he had taken the boys to town and rented a small house where they would be safe away from us. He worried about Collette and I, but knew I would refuse to leave another child of mine to fight this dreadful disease alone. Emma was only ten years old and Collette was as frail as a lark. James wanted Collette with him but also feared this because she had been exposed directly to the disease. I told him she would be of more use to me at the house and that is why she stayed with me, so that she might be my helper.

We continued in this manner for some time, me playing nursemaid to Emma Darling and Collette filling her time reading and writing poetry, working on her stitches, and taking on some of the cooking as our house staff was no longer permitted entry into our home. We were in quarantine and had a rather large "X" scrawled across our door so everyone knew not to traverse our steps.

The mood was somber as Emma grew more ill. Her cough worsened and she often gurgled up blood. Although I didn't think it possible, she lost even more weight, so that her skin hung off her sunken cheeks, dulling her once bright blue eyes. Her bones jutted out every which way, which was a startling sight. She simply couldn't take in the nutrition she needed to survive.

"Mother, will I die soon and go to heaven with Henry?" she asked me one morning while I gave her a sponge bath. I had just dipped the sponge into the warm sudsy water and started on her right shoulder, working my way down toward her elbows.

"Darling, don't speak of such things!" Blood was tinging the sputum catches more often now and I feared the worst, but refused to believe God would betray me more than once.

"But I have seen Henry, he comes and sits beside me all night long, holding my hands and rubbing my hair. He said I will know when it's time." Emma Darling didn't look afraid when she spoke of Henry's ghost, rather she looked peaceful.

"Is it time, Mother?" she repeated.

I dropped the sponge and sobbed. My once chirpy and jovial daughter was speaking to me of seeing her brother as an angel. It could only mean her time was near, for I had seen this before with my mother's passing. My beloved mother held her arms out to her husband of forty years and murmured his name before collecting her last breath and leaving us. Collette knocked at the door wanting desperately to see her sister and hold her hand in comfort while she suffered.

"Collette, please, you know I can't let you in." It pained me to deny her this gift, but it was for her benefit.

It was that evening, when I lay at Emma Darling's bedside that she began murmuring in her sleep between coughs and wheezes. "Henry?" she called out.

"Henry, the light, it's so exquisite." She continued talking softly as if Henry were right in front of her. She smiled brilliantly and took her last breath before leaving this world to be with her brother who had come for her. I felt a small measure of peace knowing they were together.

Feeling tranquil, I closed the door and went to Collette. I feared embracing her, and infecting her with Emma's disease that I was now exposed to. Who knew if one of us had it now too? Did we pick it up in town or did I miss a particle of the disease when scrubbing and scouring our home last year after Henry passed? I remembered the doctor saying it could lay dormant for years. I did not know what to do. I took selfish comfort in my remaining daughter's embrace and together we cried ourselves to sleep.

In the morning, we sent word to James and the boys that Emma had passed away. We had to spend the day in preparation for her burial, so Collette and I set to work. We decided to make a new dress for Emma's burial from the sky blue fabric she had chosen to match her eyes. I paused to wonder if the fabric could have been responsible for the transmission of the disease. I supposed anything was possible. If the disease could be airborne or originate from sputum, as I believed, then it was not only possible but likely probable.

We took measurements from Emma Darling's precious, stiffening body and set to work on her burial gown. We used the pattern she had chosen and painstakingly sewed each frilly layer together just as she would have wanted it. We spilled many tears and laughed heartily when thinking of our beloved and spent this time honoring her in the best way we knew how. I washed her body to purify it, and brushed her hair to plait. Together, Collette and I dressed her, starting with her cream-colored woolen stockings, pantaloons, shift, patent leather shoes, and finally, her new dress. We wanted her to be put in the ground in her Sunday best to meet her maker. We clasped her favorite necklace with the sterling silver cross around her neck and laid her hands by her sides.

The boys came home to mourn with us. After we prayed, James carried Emma Darling's body from her bed and placed it gently into the pint-sized casket he purchased for her final rest.

Once she was laid on the red velvet cloth that lined the coffin, we brought the boys over to say their goodbyes to their sister. We held hands around her and prayed together, then the boys took her away to be buried next to Henry on top of the hill in our meadow that overlooked the town.

Later in the evening James came back to our home alone; he settled the horses and beckoned me to walk with him. I was heartsick and vowed consumption would take no more of our children. I could no longer quell my despair and sobbed openly.

"What do we do now, James? Will you and the boys come back once I have scoured the house?" I asked, pleading with him to say yes.

"I fear for their lives, as well as Collette's, and yours too, Christine," he answered honestly.

"I will rid the house of any traces of filth, burn all the sheets, and open the windows to air it out. It will be safe again for us, husband, I need you to come home." I collapsed into his arms, as much from exhaustion as from heartbreak. I could not bear to be without his support and caresses any longer.

"The townsfolk are reporting more outbreaks and deaths. Consumption is spreading, love, and it seems no one has an answer for how to survive. But we have lost two children and we will lose no more. Prepare the house and we will come home at once." My husband held me tightly and brushed his lips against mine ever so gently. Then he tacked up his favorite pair of buggy horses and drove his carriage back into town.

CHAPTER 3

❧

THE DEPARTURE

Collette was not up with the sun the morning following Emma Darling's burial as per her normal routine. Rather than wake her, I allowed her to catch up on her sleep as we had all been through a visceral trial. My bones felt heavy and leaden from the loss but I summoned my strength and carried on as I promised and set to washing the kitchen thoroughly first and foremost. I used vats of boiling water stoked over the fire to wash down the kitchen workspace, baseboards, and then floors. Several hours passed by and still Collette had not appeared. I went to her room but her door was locked from the inside.

"Collette? Darling? Answer me." I knocked lightly at first but then panic set in and I began pounding on her door.

"Mother, don't come in, I am ill. I'm afraid I have the white plague." My daughter's voice was steady but she could not fool me, I heard the fear in her unspoken pauses.

"Collette, let me in this minute or I swear I will kick down the door if I have to." I was already backing up to wind up my kick.

"Mother, no, you must leave me be, you have the boys to think of now."

"Collette, open this door at once. I can hear that you are coughing, what else? Are you feverish?"

"I believe I am, Mother, my body aches all over. My head feels like it might split, but mostly my chest is tight and in pain." I could tell she was suffering just by the tone of her voice. I kicked the door in, not willing to wait a moment longer to see her with my own two eyes.

Just like Emma Darling, she had glassy eyes and rosy cheeks, her head was scorching and beads of sweat formed across her brow. I quickly grabbed a clean cloth and wet it with cold water from the basin, then lay it across her head to bring down her fever. When she coughed, her entire body rattled and she produced phlegm that was thick and streaked with red blood.

When James came home with the boys that evening he was met with a locked door. He knocked loudly and I met him with the grievous news. I asked him to speak to the doctor on Collette's behalf, although in my heart I already knew she had consumption.

In the morning when James returned, he told me the doctor would be by to examine our daughter later that day. I dreaded the doctor's visit and his diagnosis.

When the doctor finally made it to our home, he listened to Collette's lungs with his stethoscope. After his examination, he announced that her lymph glands were swollen to the size of grapes and that her left lung did not have good air flow. He believed that she was indeed positive for tuberculosis.

When James came by the house later that evening, he had already seen the doctor and learned of his daughter's illness. He had other news as well. The doctor knew of several sanitariums for patients with tuberculosis and was willing to write to different locations on Collette's behalf.

"I told him we will pay top dollar for Collette's care." James was a man of wealth and means and would not subject his daughter to inferior attention.

"But, James, no one will care better for Collette than I!" I protested at the thought of sending her away all alone.

"Let's see what the doctor finds out. There is even a private institution in Skaneateles, close to your family."

"Oh, let's pray then, James, let's pray to God that he provides care for her there. If that is the case, perhaps I could stay with my sister, if she would allow it." My sister had a large house with ample room for me.

"I will return in the morning with more food and advice from Dr. Hill, but it will be several days, perhaps a week even, until we know if there is room in Skaneateles." James stood in the doorway, tears filling his tormented eyes, as he said goodbye to me once more.

While Collette slept, I took advantage of the quiet and closed my eyes, hoping to catch some sleep on my own feather bed. I thought of how perfect our life was just one year ago, we were all so merry and full of *joie de vivre* and then suddenly everything changed.

I wondered about the sanitariums. How could they provide any better standard of care for my daughter than I already was? I kept her cool, pounded her back, attended her bowels, collected her spit, and analyzed it for change. I even kept a diary with her daily symptoms and any changes or progresses she felt from day to day.

There was no cure for consumption. Perhaps keeping Collette comfortable was the most important thing I could do now. I fell into a fitful slumber and woke with renewed fervor and hope. God was not punishing us, he was carrying us through our difficulty and through him, we would survive.

In the morning, James returned with fresh fruit and bread from the market. I thanked him for I hadn't time to cook or clean; only to tend to Collette.

"Dr. Hill has told me more about the sanitarium in Skaneateles. It only has room for six individuals, it's a private residence where a doctor looks in upon the patients daily. The homeowner takes care of the patients the rest of the time. He's not sure if there is a bed available for Collette, but seeing as the woman is doing all the work alone, he suggested we offer your services as a means of entry."

"Why certainly. I am willing to go and tend Collette. Even if she has a doctor who checks in on her daily, I imagine I could still be helpful in other ways. What about you and the boys? What will you do?" I searched my husband's eyes for answers.

"The boys and I will rent a house in town and we will be fine, Christine. It's you I worry about."

"I have shown no signs of the plague so far, James, I will be fine. Collette will remain alive, just get her a room!"

The basket of fruit James brought contained oranges, bananas, and fresh strawberries. I held the navel orange to my nose and inhaled its sweet musty scent. I was re-energized at once and made a small bowl of the berries and mashed them for Collette. Her throat was sore, and it was difficult to eat solid foods. When I approached her bedroom, I could hear her tiny whimper, the pathetic sound of her whistling lungs reached my ears from across the hallway.

"Let's prop you up further, dear." I fluffed my daughter's pillows and put her into a sitting position, cocooning her legs and torso as the doctor ordered. She was positioned by the window and the sunlight shone in on her, lifting her mood, forcing a smile. The doctor in town referred to this as heliotherapy and promised, if nothing else, the sunlight would lift our spirits.

"I have made you a berry mash. Can you eat it yourself?" I asked, before treating my daughter like an invalid.

"I will try," Collette said. She removed one arm from the cocoon and began lifting the mash to her mouth with shaky concentration. She was shivering and frail, and even the tiniest exertion left her spent. I took over the task of feeding her, not wishing to insult her dignity, but needing to get nutrition into her body so she didn't waste away. Her bowel movements were only coming once every three days now, and she was growing thinner.

After eating and bathing, we sat together, looking out the window at the glorious sunshine, and the flurry of activity caused by the birds and bunnies below. The scene was captivating.

"Can I get you anything, Collette, maybe some drawing paper and an inkwell? You could do a sketch or create a story from what you see out your window?" I intended to renew her with hope and vigor, but she was placid and quiet.

"No thank you, Mother, I will just enjoy watching for now," she blinked a few times, then let her eyes close while she rested.

I gathered her chamber pot and set about emptying it. Upon my return, I cleaned her room of lingering dust mites and tidied up a bit. Then I left her to rest, and she slept rather well considering her cough.

In between cleaning and disinfecting the homestead, I began filling a small suitcase in the event we were lucky enough to find a bed. The journey would not be long; we estimated it to be about one hundred twenty miles, James could visit monthly with any items we needed. For now, I laundered and packed my own dressing gown, several aprons, and dresses, pairs of stockings, underwear, and slippers. I also set aside several skeins of yarn and multiple sizes of knitting needles to take for when I was idle. I would require paper and pen to correspond with James and the boys, several bottles of ink, and that left me wondering about food. I would ask James if food was to be provided as well. I could always offer to help cook. I was not a wizard in the kitchen, but I could make basic soups and breads with ease.

The morning came with news. The doctor was able to secure a room for Collette beginning in two days' time in Skaneateles. I needed to pack her belongings and tell her about our journey. All James knew was what he had previously explained; I would go along with my daughter to a private residence that held six patients. The six patients would be under the care of Dr. William Kennedy, a well-respected doctor in the town of Skaneateles. My duties were not clear, but I would learn them upon our arrival. I didn't know where I would reside but, hopefully, close to my daughter.

"Collette, I have some news," I spoke gently and stroked her palms with my thumbs as I held them in my own.

"What is it, Mama?" she only called me "mama" when she was nervous and frightened.

"We have secured a place for you in a home for tuberculosis patients. There will be a doctor to see you daily, and best of all, I get to come with you."

"But, Mama, why must I leave? I am feeling better, truly. I haven't spit blood in several days and I will eat more, I promise!" She was borderline hysterical.

"I know you are trying, dear, but this home will provide you with better care than I can. A doctor tend you every day, Collette, to help ease your suffering and perhaps even make you well again."

"Mama…," she cried openly now.

"I know it's not what Henry and Emma did, but now there is more hope for cure and treatments. We have to try them, you won't be alone. I will be by your side every moment."

Choking back her tears, she asked, "When do we leave then?" resolved to the fact we were leaving regardless of her input.

"We leave in two days. I will start your laundry and packing. Is there anything special you'd like to bring?"

"Something of Emma's perhaps? To remind me of her?" her eyes darted toward Emma Darling's desk and settled on her stack of books.

"Okay, how about her diary from Christmas? Perhaps you can fill it in for her where she left off?" Emma Darling's diary was a gorgeous red leather bound book with a large cursive letter 'E' stamped into the cover. A tassel that acted as a bookmark hung down the side.

"Yes, I would like that." Collette began a coughing fit that lasted the better part of thirty minutes. She coughed sputum and blood, thick chunks, as she had not done before. I was anxious to have her under a doctor's care now and grateful we had the means to secure a place.

The following morning Collette woke with a raging fever. She had no appetite and was completely fatigued and drained from all that her body suffered throughout the night. Her body was drenched with sweat, tingeing it with an odor so that by the morning she required a fresh sponge bath. Her chest pain remained constant, and she coughed repeatedly. We needed a remedy quickly or I feared for the loss of this daughter as well. She was the weakest child of all five; she was always sickly, and yet somehow she had survived worse symptoms than either Henry or Emma. Henry and Emma presented with cough and pain, but went more quickly into a drowning of sorts; their lungs could not sustain all the fluid that built up. But Collette was able to express more sputum and somehow this was keeping her alive.

The morning of our departure, the boys came to the yard, and while they kept their distance from us, they waved and smiled, wishing us safe travels and better health. They promised to write and James had a bundle of stationery that he bought special for us as a parting gift. We did not embrace but we held one another's gaze longingly, our life together but a blink of an eye, all we built, the family we created, narrowed down now and torn apart.

"I love you!" I yelled to my husband and boys as the driver of our tidy governess carriage pulled away from our home.

"We love you!" the boys called back to Collette and me, waving at us as we descended over the hilltop down into the valley below.

We would need their love and appreciate it daily, for what lie ahead was a scary prospect.

CHAPTER 4

꧁❦꧂

SUMMERTIME IN SKANEATELES

Our journey to the sanitarium was long and tiresome. The governess cart was smaller than a normal carriage and had a black bench that only seated two patrons. The coachman sat directly in front of us. Still, it was spacious enough for us to stretch our legs. Collette enjoyed the scenery and fresh outdoor air until the wind kicked up and her coughing took over. I wrapped her head and mouth in a linen scarf decorated with tiny rosebuds, but the air was warm, making it hard to breathe through the material. My daughter preferred the crisp cool air to the summer heat, and summer was on its way.

We were delivered to a village home with a wraparound front porch, where we were met by the woman who ran the facility, Marjorie Putnam.

"Pleased to meet you. You must be Christine and Collette Lyndon." She reached out and shook both of our hands. I took note immediately that she was not afraid to touch Collette.

"The pleasure is ours, Mrs. Putnam. Thank you very much for providing a space for Collette," I remarked.

"She will do well here, I am sure of it. Let's get you inside and acquainted with the space. You know there are five other individuals here, all women. You are the youngest though, so there is no one else your age to pass the time with, I am afraid," she muttered as she helped carry our small parcel of bags inside.

"Oh it's lovely," I exclaimed as I looked about the home. It was larger than it appeared from the outside and was immaculate. The walls were painted a soft blue and creamy butter color throughout the house, engendering a sense of calm.

"Thank you, I do my best to keep it tidy, and now that I have you here to help I can get even more done. I do appreciate having your help, you know, it can get tiring." The woman led us through the drawing room and down a corridor to a set of rooms.

"Whatever you need from me, please just let me know," I said, but looking about the home everything seemed in control.

"I will, but tonight, you will rest. Collette, this will be your bed, I rather hoped you would enjoy being in the back of the house overlooking the lake. Your mother will be in the room beside you, the spaces are small as you'll see, but they are efficient. You'll spend most of your time resting on the porch any way, as the doctor thinks the outdoor air helps loosen the mucus."

Collette rested on her bed while I unpacked her few treasures that we brought. I put Emma Darling's diary on top of the bedside table along with a pen. The view from her room was splendid; the sun danced off the lake and brought about a feeling of peace. The sanitarium was not far from my sister's home, but she did not wish to see me while we were harbingers. She had her own family to protect and I understood this all too well.

I allowed Collette to sleep while I prepared my own room. I made up my bed; it had a firm mattress just as I liked, and I unpacked my dresses and undergarments into the side drawer that was provided. Then I took time to walk around the property and meet the other inhabitants.

All the women were propped side by side on lounge chairs overlooking the lake. Sylvia was twenty-two; she had been here the longest and was faring well. Maria was twenty-five, had already lost two children to the disease, and looked very forlorn; her cough was deep and productive. I worried about her. Andrea was thirty-one years old, had never been married, and seemed to be the type that hated being fawned over. Then there were Milly and Sarah, both women in their late thirties, seemingly very dear friends. They shared a stack of books between them and worried over one another like a couple of old hens. These ladies had been here over a year now; their coughs had diminished, but they still grew fatigued rapidly.

I helped Marjorie prepare the dinner meal and she and I served the patients, cleaned the dishes, and then we sat together and ate.

"The soup is wonderful, Marjorie. I am sure Collette will enjoy it; I will just let her sleep a little longer. Am I tasting mint?" I asked.

"Yes, I keep a garden of herbs in the back. I just love mint with cucumber soup, it's so refreshing, and the girls all like it well enough. Tell me about Collette then, and her suffering."

"Well, first I suppose I should tell you that I have lost two children already. Collette is my third to come down with the plague, but she has lasted the longest. She has always suffered with poor health, was never able to skip and play like my other children without becoming winded on account of her asthma. Now her stomach addles her, and she often has diarrhea and skin rashes. So, how she has survived this long I can only guess is by the grace of God."

"Amen, I do believe that," Marjorie chimed in.

"Collette is patient and calm, not one for complaining or wishing her life away. She takes what is given and carries on. She is afraid that I will get sick too, but I have been exposed to this for over a year so I think I am safe." I spooned another mouthful of the savory soup into my mouth and let it linger on my tongue before swallowing. Martha, our cook for twenty years, had never prepared a cold soup and I rather enjoyed it.

"Well, it can lay dormant for years within your system, and it doesn't attack everyone in the same way. All of these ladies are typical tuberculosis patients whose disease is manifested in the lungs, dramatically compromising them. However, you can also develop the disease in your nervous system, debilitating your ability to walk and keep control over your bodily functions. Or you can have bilious tuberculosis, which makes one very nauseous and causes vomiting. Then there is lymphatic tuberculosis whose effects begin in childhood, causing painful swelling in the neck, infection in the lymph nodes, anemia, low weight, and fatigue. Finally, there is the sanguineous form of the disease that affects the skeletal system by adhering to the bone."

"My Lord in heaven, I had no idea there were different kinds. Are you a nurse? Is that how you know so much and how you have kept yourself safe?" I was amazed by this woman's knowledge base and wanted to learn as much as I could from her.

"The Lord called me to be a nurse many years ago. I pray every night that I remain healthy so that I might help ease the pain and suffering of those I am meant to care for."

"I do the same. I am healthy, and until otherwise, I will not waste a minute of my time worrying I will become ill. I have two boys and a husband at home. I intend to help Collette get better and then move back home to be a family once more."

"I will put you in my prayers, Christine. It's getting late, there is more cold cucumber soup in the refrigerator for Collette. Please be sure she eats. If you can be up by six in the morning, you can help me start breakfast for the ladies. The doctor comes by nine o'clock, so we try to have our meal and bath before his arrival."

"Certainly, Marjorie. You are doing a wonderful thing here. I hope we can be friends."

"We already are!" she stated and left me behind to check on her patients once more before turning into bed herself.

Marjorie was a remarkable and charismatic woman who ran the sanitarium as tight as a ship. Next to each patient's bed was a clipboard with schedules and notations. Every meal was detailed along with how much the patient ate. Each bowel movement was noted and described as loose, normal, or otherwise. Body chemistries were taken as well as blood pressures and heart rates. These were repeated and charted every four hours on the dot. Additionally, Marjorie noted what books the patient had already read, and what was on their wish list. She had a rotating system in her house and always made sure her patients had something to occupy their mind. She felt if their minds wandered they would fall into depression or worse, they would lose all hope and, finally, the will to live.

"Good morning, Collette. How do you feel today, darling?" I stepped quietly into my daughter's room and was happy to find her awake.

"I feel nervous, Mother. What if the other women don't like me?"

"Don't be silly, I have met them all, and they are very welcoming. Several have offered their books and drawing pads to you for entertainment already. Besides, we are here to get you better, not to make friends." I felt a pang of guilt for saying this, but it was the truth after all.

I walked Collette from her bedroom to her lounge chair, which was positioned on the porch with a lakeside view that today included several sailboats. She coughed profusely from walking the short distance but once settled into her seat, she calmed. I showed her the spittoon beside her lounge chair and told her that I would be by with breakfast momentarily.

I hoped Marjorie would teach me to take blood pressures so that I could take one or two patients under my care entirely.

I met up with Marjorie in the kitchen and together we prepared the morning meal of scrambled eggs and toast for each of the ladies. Marjorie explained that the doctor believed a diet high in protein, especially dairy products, supplied the women with the type of nutrition they needed when infected with the plague.

I put several steaming hot plates on a large tray and carried them onto the porch. I was tickled to see the other women walking toward Collette and greeting her warmly, making her feel welcome.

"Good morning, ladies," I chimed, "how is everyone today?" I forced a smile to my lips, not allowing myself to wallow in my own losses and circumstances.

Sylvia and Maria seemed to be doing well; they had good color and hearty appetites. The other women pushed the food around on their plates and only nibbled at their toast. All the women were thin, too thin.

Andrea was coughing profusely and had perspiration covering her skin. She would be first in line with the doctor today. Marjorie told me she had been getting worse over the past few weeks, and she was concerned. We needed to obtain her weight today to see whether she was thriving.

Milly and Sarah, the pair of hens, clucked at one another to eat more, and finish their milk, but neither did.

I helped Collette eat, for she was very shaky both from nerves and exhaustion. I managed to get a solid egg into her, and she drank half her milk, so I was pleased.

After breakfast, we bathed the women with as much dignity as we could. We kept all parts of their bodies clothed except the spot we washed. The porch was extremely private and often the women just gazed out onto the lake while being bathed. Thankfully, they had something beautiful to pass the time with.

"Christine, the doctor is here and wishes to speak with you," Marjorie announced.

"Good morning, sir, I am Christine Lyndon, Collette's mother. It's nice to meet you," I said, admiring the man who took such grand care of these ladies.

"Lovely to meet you too, although the circumstances are difficult. I am going to give Collette a full physical, in the privacy of her room, and she would like you to be present." The doctor was older, in his fifties; he wore framed glasses and a stethoscope around his neck. His demeanor was very soothing, and I had no worries he would frighten Collette.

"Certainly." I followed the doctor, who carried his leather satchel, into my daughter's room.

"Collette, I am Dr. Kennedy. I am going to give you a full physical now to determine your origin of pain, which includes everything, even your eyes and ears. Okay?"

"Yes, sir," Collette agreed stoically.

Once the exam was over, the doctor retreated to the kitchen table, his denoted office space. Marjorie and I left him to his notes and charts. We walked among the women on the porch, now including Collette, and offered new books, drawing pads, and beverages. Each lady was occupied for the time being, so I began making up the beds as instructed by Marjorie. The ladies had personalized their tiny bedrooms with photos from home; several had letters and artifacts as well. I made a note to myself to ask James to send the photograph from last Christmas when the entire family was together.

Marjorie asked me to walk into town and pick up some groceries for her. She gave me a specific list, and I was more than happy to run the errand. While on the way, I came across a man with a racking cough who spit several times on the ground. He had no notion this was unsanitary, and I was appalled. I went about my errands but upon my return, both Marjorie and the doctor could tell I had been riled up. I told them what took place and explained the spittoons and laws we had put in place in Pittsford against spitting. They were impressed the town took such an active role in the health of its inhabitants and wished Skaneateles would do the same.

"I will see to it then. Tell me who the mayor is and I will schedule a meeting at once," I said, setting in motion my crusade to end tuberculosis.

I met with the mayor as well as the chief of police; the doctor came along with me to several meetings and together we devised rules for the town. Similar to the rules in Pittsford, spitting was now strictly banned. We took funds from the town's treasury to purchase spittoons for each village corner. Restaurateurs were encouraged to purchase their own. Errand boys were hired to burn any hankies or napkins disposed of by lungers. Signs were posted that read off the rules for the anti-spitting campaign.

On Sunday morning, I went to church with Marjorie; it was the one and only time she left her patients unattended. She needed the respite the service provided and only left if the patients were in satisfactory condition. We walked the quarter-mile to worship and found the church half empty upon our arrival. Patrons were either afraid to come to worship and fall ill, or they already had. I spoke with the minister after worship hours and offered my services to check on ill patients. He was grateful and gave me a list of seven individuals who he knew were sick and could not afford proper medical treatment.

That afternoon I set about with an errand boy who drove me by horse and buggy to visit several patients. What I found astounded me. The first home bore witness to the horrors of this disease. The family that once boasted six children now only had two alive. The mother had passed away and the father was ill and unable to take care of the little ones. The stench of loose bowels overwhelmed the home and the suffering was palpable. The children had fevers and a great deal of chest pain; they had chalky lips, coughed blood, and were white as ghosts. The father did not fare much better. I propped them in their beds beside the windows and opened the doors to allow for better airflow. I promised to be back in the morning with food and help.

The other individuals I checked in on were faring much the same. Entire homes were devastated by the disease and my third house was more than I could bear. I knocked gently at first but when no one answered, I allowed myself entry. The smell of death hit my nose immediately. Walking through the rooms, I found the source. Two small children lay cuddled together on a cot, both passed on to a better, more peaceful place. I continued my search and found the mother also passed on, but the father was alive, ailing but alive. He had no energy to bury his family and knew he was next in line. I escorted him out of his hovel and onto the porch, dragging an empty cot with me. I lay him down, propping him with pillows and patted his back repeatedly. I assured him I would tend to the rest.

By the time I had visited each of the seven families I was tired and overwhelmed by the promises I made. I had to recruit help. I would speak with Marjorie and the doctor about this as soon as possible.

❊

"Marjorie, I had no idea it was so widespread here. The little ones are all alone with no food in their refrigerators, and they are terrified for their lives. It's heartbreaking." I felt tears welling in the corners of my eyes as I recounted my findings.

"Oh my goodness. That is dire. It seems we will need a lot of help."

"Who can we recruit? I will write at once to my sister and see if any of her charitable organizations can provide meals or funding. Perhaps we can ask the doctor if any of his nurses from the hospital would be willing to make rounds?"

"Yes, and perhaps the churches or the service clubs can also sponsor some individuals. Here, take some paper and let's draft a letter to everyone we can think of. We can't just let these people die."

"I promised them all a return tomorrow. I apologize, Marjorie. I know it was wrong of me. I am here to help you, but when I saw how dire their circumstances, I couldn't stand to leave them unattended."

"You did the right thing. I will go on attending the ladies, as we have things under control here. You tend to the families in need, starting tomorrow. Let's rise at five o'clock sharp and begin breakfast for them. How many individuals shall we account for?"

"Well, in my travels, I found fourteen people still among the living. A few may not make it through the night though."

"Okay, let's prepare three dozen hard-boiled eggs and bread with butter for them. I have the supplies on hand, but tomorrow we will have to restock."

"I can do that on my way home," I volunteered, not quite certain what I had gotten myself into.

That evening, before I lay my head to rest, I spoke to Collette about what I had found. She was devastated that so many people lay dying without help and doctors.

"What can I do?" she asked, wanting to help.

"I wondered about your lovely sketches; perhaps we can sell them in town for charity?" Collette had heightened artistic abilities as compared to other children. She paid close attention to detail, which brought her images to life.

"Oh yes, Mother, that would be wonderful! I will start my drawings tomorrow; I have sketched one of the lake already, and will make many more."

I hoped that drawing the lake would be therapeutic in and of itself, but now that her drawings could act as means to raise charity funds, it would be healing, as well.

"I will write at once to your father for more supplies and suggest he and the boys can even handle the sale."

"I feel guilty, Mother, guilty for my good fortune," she swept a tear across her face and stifled a sob.

"There, there, we will help anyone who needs us how ever we can so that everyone has the same chance at a good outcome." This was my fervent promise.

When I finally lay my head to rest that evening I was spent, still my mind wandered and sleep eluded me. I thought of additional ways to fundraise, starting with a book sale, then perhaps a bake sale. I would write again to my sister and ask for more help. So far, she remained unscathed by the disease, but that could change.

In the weeks that followed, Marjorie and I instituted prayer lines and we used the kitchen at the Presbyterian church as the home base for meal preparation. Dozens of volunteers organized the preparation and distribution of the morning meals, beginning with families in this parish but quickly extending to anyone in need. Dozens of people were afflicted and unable to care for themselves. Marjorie's was the only sanitarium in town and many of the town's folk did not have the means to travel elsewhere.

Dr. Kennedy recruited volunteers from the hospital; I held these particular volunteers in high esteem, as they were willing to put themselves in harm's way. Their task was to visit with the patients, clean messes, empty bed pans, feed and bath those who needed it, as well as coddle the children. Financial assistance came in, and at least for now, we managed to purchase enough food supplies to continue our campaign.

My husband and sons held a sidewalk sale in front of the grocery store; they sold Collette's colored sketches of the lake in all its glory, as well as knit objects that were donated. Books were sold, and many hundreds more were donated to create a larger circulating library at Marjorie's home. It was exciting to be part of such an enormous campaign. It was energizing and liberating too.

"We owe it all to you, Christine. Without you, we would not have had the foresight to take care of our own as you have taught us," Marjorie admitted, as she counted the money we had taken in.

"Well, we owe it to the lunger who spit before me all those weeks ago then. He appalled me so much and made me think about Henry's death. I just wanted to prevent another mother from losing her son senselessly."

"The rules are set now. Everyone seems to be following them, and the town is invested in everyone's health and well-being. They are even giving checkups at the schools," Dr. Kennedy interjected.

"Christine, do you feel okay?" Marjorie asked that evening after discussing our successes at gathering funds.

"Just a little tired is all. I think I will turn in early tonight if you don't mind." The day had gotten the best of me indeed.

"I don't mind at all. Take care of yourself first, Christine, or you're no good to anyone else," she sent me on my way with a gentle nudge.

By the morning, I still felt the weight of fatigue. I was nauseous as well and had trouble completing my own breakfast meal. That's when I realized I hadn't bled yet this month. Oh, no, I was several weeks, six to be precise, past my menstrual cycle. In fact, I skipped an entire month and was typically as regular as clockwork. My nipples were slightly sore, and I admitted I had a glow. I had noticed the shine on my face last week but attributed it to all the hard work I was undertaking.

I counted back to the last time James and I were together. Sure enough, it was right before Collette and I arrived here a month and a half ago at the beginning of June. I had been so preoccupied with caring for the ladies and now campaigning for the townsfolk that I hardly paid attention to my physical self. Hand across my belly, I was certain I was with child.

"Marjorie, when will the doctor be here today, did he say?" I asked as we prepared breakfast for the ladies.

"His usual time of nine o'clock. Dear, you look peeked. Sit and let me get you some tea."

"Thank you, Marjorie." I let my friend prepare my tea, two sugars, one cream, and hemmed and hawed over telling her my news.

"What's on your mind?" she asked. It was five a.m. and we had a few moments to chat before getting started with our food contributions to the town as well as our own patients.

"Would you believe it if I told you I am pregnant?"

"Ha!" she laughed out loud and clapped her hands in excitement.

"You think this is a good thing then?" I asked, somewhat bewildered.

"I do! It will be wonderful to bring new life into this world. Oh, your husband will be so happy, won't he?"

"Goodness, I hope so. I need to speak to the doctor at once. What type of risk am I imposing on my unborn child by being among so many who are ill?" I wondered.

"Well, I recall the baby has your immune system during gestation and hopefully, because you are healthy, the baby is as well."

"Is that true? I hope you are right. I just don't know how I will take care of a baby as well as Collette. It's a precarious situation to be in. I suppose I have time to figure that out."

"Yes, you do, seven and a half months to be precise. Oh, golly, I wonder if it's a boy or girl." Marjorie started humming to herself as she did whenever she was happy. She cracked eggs with one hand into the frying pan and began whisking them together. I watched her joy emerge and allowed myself to feel it too.

When the doctor arrived, he spoke with me about my situation. He had a colleague who specialized in female care and would make the necessary appointment for me. He believed the disease to be infectious, but would confer with this other doctor to determine my safety. I wouldn't leave Collette, he and Marjorie both knew that, but now we had someone else to think of.

CHAPTER 5

❦

AUTUMN

Sadly, we lost Maria in the fall. She was a gentle soul who grew worse after she refused the pulmonary lobectomy Dr. Kennedy recommended. She had already endured the torment of the pneumothorax on her left lung. The doctor hoped that by collapsing it for a time it would allow itself to heal. Instead, Maria grew feverish and struggled more with her breathing as her body was no longer efficient enough to circulate air. Her vital organs gave way and she passed on while Marjorie held her hands. Although Maria was the most private patient among the ladies, she allowed everyone to be by her side in her last moments. Everyone took comfort in the moment, finally knowing she was at peace in heaven with her daughters by her side.

My pregnancy lifted everyone's spirits after Maria's passing. My belly grew rather large and I waddled now when I walked, which became a laughing joke. The doctor administered an osculation exam where he listened for fetal movement. He felt I was safe for now but when the baby came I would need to send him or her home with James since being among ill ladies was not wise.

"Mother, let me feel the baby kick again," Collette spoke in a whisper.

I walked toward her, jutting my large belly in front of her as she lie positioned upright on the porch. I was five months along by October and feeling strong and healthy. The baby was a good kicker, and very large in comparison to my others. I carried this one higher in my belly as well.

"I felt it!" she exclaimed and then launched into a coughing fit. She spit up half a cup of mucus and all of it was lined with blood. The air by the lake was no longer helping her the way it did initially. Her cheeks were flushed once more and her appetite had waned substantially. If not for the baby and her charity work to keep her alive, I don't know if she would still be among us. She sold dozens of her sketches and donated every penny to the tuberculosis campaign established under her name in town. The funds provided meals, clothing, and medical care for anyone in need, regardless of their parish or station in life. Collette had a purpose and it was sustaining her.

After the doctor examined her today, he had concerns.

"She is no longer thriving in this environment, Christine. I can do a pneumothorax on her as I did on Maria, but would advise against it. She is too frail for that. She is losing more weight, suffers from night sweats, has no appetite, and is exhausted all the time."

"I know, doctor, what more can we do for her? I will pay anything," I pleaded.

"It's not about the money, it's about the environment. I have been researching and found another sanitarium that may be more beneficial to her."

"Where is it, doctor, and how is it different or better than this one, with you right close by?"

"It's in the Adirondack Mountains, led by Doctor Edward Livingston Trudeau. He lost his own brother to the disease and had it himself, but now he seems controlled."

"How is that possible?"

"He attributes it to the clean and, more importantly, cool mountain air. He believes, as I do, in the rest cure. His patients line the porches of the buildings and take in the crisp air for eight hours a day, reclining and resting only."

"But how do we know if it will work for Collette?"

"We don't, but it may be the best option. There are places you can take her in the desert, some people think the dry air approach is more hospitable for patients, or you can try the sea air. Some people believe that halotherapy is the only way to control tuberculosis because the salty air is said to decrease inflammation."

"Well, what do you think?"

"I think the mountain air would be best for her. I will write a letter on your behalf if you wish."

"Thank you, doctor, if that's what you advise, then I suppose it's what's best for Collette."

I wrote straight away to James telling him the news. He was very attentive to our letters and most often wrote back the same day as receiving them. In this case, he planned a visit to Skaneateles to speak with me in person. When he arrived, he stood several yards from me, we didn't hold hands or embrace, but he admired my growing belly and looked pleased with himself.

"Tell me about the sanitarium the doctor recommends."

"Well there is a doctor there who only sees tuberculosis patients. In fact, he studies them too. Apparently, it is quite a set up. There are numerous cottages for patients; I suppose they are more like homes. There is a chapel and a building for occupational therapy. The humidity is low and the sunshine abundant even in the winter months, but more importantly, the doctor is now cured of the disease, James. Think of it. What if we can cure Collette?"

"I can think of nothing better. I say we try it. You will be farther away from us of course, and you won't have your sister's family close by."

"I know. It has been nice seeing more of them since they've become involved in the campaign against consumption. They do a lot of the fundraising, and for that, I am grateful. But it isn't as if we visit one another and spend a lot of time together. The people we will miss the most are you and the boys."

"When do you expect to receive word if there is a bed available?"

"Dr. Kennedy feels certain there is a bed available; the place is rather large, providing for dozens of patients already. There are children too, which will be nice for Collette."

"What about the baby, who will take care of you there? You had a plan in place here."

"I spoke to the doctor about that. I have three and a half more months in my term. He feels I can travel safely and get Collette established. Then I will travel home to give birth and nurse the baby for a few weeks. You will have to line up a wet nurse, James, and a nanny to care for her. Choose someone kind and nurturing."

"Yes, I have begun looking into that already. When will you leave?"

"As soon as the doctor receives confirmation that we can go. I will offer my services once more and hope to help as I have here."

"Saranac Lake, huh, it sounds like a pretty place at least."

"Yes, it does," I agreed, praying it really was.

CHAPTER 6

❧

SARANAC LAKE

"The land was all donated by Indian guides and residents of the village," Dr. Trudeau said as he gestured to the sixteen acres of vast land around us. Fields scattered with wild dandelions were intersected by robust, streaming creeks that wound their way down the mountainside, through the gorges and gullies slick with yellowing moss. Meadows, teaming with life, were matted down where the deer slept at night. Wild lilies and yarrow clumped around the deciduous trees that the squirrels and chipmunks scampered on, leaping from branch to branch. They shook a carpet of scarlet, plum, and golden leaves upon the ground as they frantically searched and stored their food for the long winter months that lie ahead. Mountains tipped with white caps could be seen in the distance; it was a beautiful sight. This was Saranac Lake, our new peaceful, yet vibrant, home.

"That was generous," I stated, already liking this man even though we had just met. He was warm and empathetic; what's more, the property was magnificent, stealing my breath for a moment. Moving onward, he pointed out a small cottage on the outskirts of the land that was built in the middle of a field surrounded by asters that were going to seed.

"Little Red housed our first patients several years ago. They were a set of sisters who were factory workers in New York. I believe that the cottage-like structures maximize the patient's exposure to the clean air. The sunlight and scenery help them escape the boredom they all experience." He walked by a small red outbuilding that was very charming. It was his first structure and cost three hundred and fifty dollars to build. He admitted that is was more cost effective to raise the money for one small structure at a time rather than large institution-like structures, which he didn't like anyway because of their sanitation difficulties.

We walked past the "Little Red" amidst a light snowfall, which was not unusual this time of year in the mountains, and onward toward several other buildings. My dress swept across the fluffy snowflakes on the ground like a broom across a dusty floor. First, the doctor pointed out the "nursing cottages" where the particularly weak patients stayed. Second, he noted the boarding houses and cottages for the more ambulatory patients. Third, he showed me the cottages devised for specific populations, for instance the Greeks inhabited one home while the Cubans, blacks, and kosher Jews each had their own. People were even further separated by occupation; there was a cottage for circus people, one for telephone workers, employees of DuPont, as well as employees of Endicott Johnson Shoes. He wanted his sanitarium to be different, he wanted a place where people with little purse could come and find peace among the balsam-scented forest and isolation of everyday stresses.

Dr. Trudeau showed me the central kitchen and laundry facilities as well as his personal office space. I was intrigued by the guinea pigs he kept in a special pit behind his desk. They were warmed by a lantern and he used them as specimens in his study of the disease. He used coagulated sheep's blood to culture bacteria, inject the pigs, and watch for development of disease.

I offered my services immediately to help in the research of the disease.

"It's not very glamorous. The research involves collecting spit every morning from each and every patient, then examining it for change and recording the findings. In addition, you would have to inoculate the pigs and rabbits and watch for disease."

"I can do that, doctor. I need to do something to help, to feel I am earning my stay." My voice cracked, deceiving even me and indicating to the doctor that I was not entirely together after all.

"Well, then, I will show you all the animals in the cellar and tell you about some of my experiments to date and we can go from there."

"Very well, when shall we have our first meeting?" I asked eager to get an assignment and start work.

"Once you have your daughter settled in nicely and you are settled yourself we will discuss the experimentation and what it involves. However, until the baby is born we will give you a desk job, keeping charts and statistical data." He was more than happy to hand over some of his tedious paperwork.

"Fair enough, doctor." I replied, my hand protectively resting across my belly.

"When is the baby due?" he asked cautiously.

"She is due in eight or nine weeks, I had hoped to go home for the birth, but perhaps you know of a doctor or midwife here who can help me in my delivery?" I hovered at the doorway, noting the low storm clouds that approached.

"As a matter of fact I do, I will schedule an appointment for you."

"Thank you, doctor," I said.

"I have children of my own you know, and a wife, Lottie. I am sure she will look forward to meeting you. I will coordinate an appointment for you with her midwife so you can get acquainted. My wife is from New York City and we have a home there where she spends a lot of time. We have a daughter Charlotte, whom we call Chatte. She attends a girls school in New York City. I have a son Ned, but sadly, my son Henry passed away. He was sickly for a brief time the winter of '78 and never fully recovered. He passed away peacefully in his crib."

"Oh, I am sorry to hear that."

"Yes, well, my wife is rather deliberate; she meets life's struggles head on and then moves forward. Our fourth child is due in the spring."

"Congratulations, then, I wish you all the best."

"I can see that you miss your family. I miss my family too. I have tried numerous times to move permanently back to the city house for the summers, but every time I do, I relapse. Now Saranac Lake is my permanent home," he explained.

"So we are both living apart from the ones we love then?" I realized.

"Yes, I suppose we are for the time being, but the time goes by quickly, and before I know it summer is over and once more my family is by my side. The children enroll in school and Lottie helps me care for the animals in the cellar. I am a hunter in my spare time; I collect animal specimens to study. It would be against my conscience to leave at this point in time no matter what. Besides, I have grown to love it here. When I first arrived and began taking patients, throngs of people would show up on my doorstep, line my pathway, and fill my yard. There were no appropriate accommodations at the time, and I couldn't turn these ill folks away. That is why we formed a committee and began construction, and look at us now. The "Sans," as we call it, is up and running quite well."

"Of course it's not my business, but I should think it cost you a small fortune, doctor. I, for one, am most grateful for your generosity."

Patients at the Sans paid a minimal fee as outlined in our contract, but because I was helping, our fee was whittled down even further.

"Oh, as I said earlier, the land, all sixteen acres, was donated by local guides and residents. Many of the friends I made while staying at Paul Smith's Hotel financed the cause, in fact Anson Phelps Stokes gave five hundred dollars to the cause in cash."

"The New York banker? That Anson Stokes?" I asked, having heard from James about this wealthy businessman.

"He can afford it. Not all of the sanitarium has been built from donations, however, we also raise charitable funds ourselves. It's a semi-charitable institution, I suppose you could say."

"I did quite a bit of fundraising while in Skaneateles, I would be happy to help with that as well."

"Wonderful, I am sure your services will come in quite handy then. Many of the volunteers are family members of the sick and they have no experience. Next on our agenda is the establishment of a nursing school specific to the needs of patients with tuberculosis. I have also proposed to the board that we offer a program for physicians as well, a six-week course that would allow them to learn from our established treatment protocol. All in good time I suppose."

"Well, anything I can do, Dr. Trudeau, I am at your service. I better go see to Collette now. Thank you for showing me around."

"One more thing, Christine, well, two actually." The doctor retreated into a small closet within his office for a moment and returned with a small pillow that smelled of the outdoors. He also had a pamphlet of rules.

"This is a balsam pillow. The patients make them by filling a sack with balsam pitch and sugar. Then they sew them together and make them look pretty." He noted the ruffled lace edge around the pillow he held out to me.

"What's it for?" I asked, bringing it to my nose and inhaling the sweet, fragrant scent.

"It should go under Collette's head at night to make her breathing easier. It's just one of the remedies we use, passed on to us from the Indian guides I met here long ago. As for the pamphlet, I am not worried about you and your daughter breaking any of our rules, it's more of a guidebook, but if you'd glance at it and sign it, I will put it in your file."

"Thank you, I am sure Collette will enjoy the scent as I do. We will be sure to sign the rule book this evening and return it to you tomorrow." I left the doctor with feelings of gratitude, and confidence that Collette would receive wonderful treatment under this man's care.

When I found Collette, she was seated on a porch overlooking a mountain stream, bunnies hopped about, birds flitted here and there, and squirrels gathered nuts for the upcoming winter. Best of all, other young ladies her age were beside her in lounge chairs. She was seventeen now and hadn't enjoyed company from young ladies her own age in over a year. She was showing the other patients her watercolor sketches from Skaneateles and telling them about the fundraising we did there. She hoped to find new images to render and sell once more, perhaps in Saranac Lake.

The town was growing as more and more patients and their families moved here. It made me think of James. We had the means to purchase a village home; he and the boys, and the baby, would be close to us if they were willing to make a change. I would write to him as promised once we were unpacked, and put the bug in his ear.

I wandered into my own quarters; the doctor placed me in a small building for staff. I had a bed and side table as well as use of the small kitchenette and dining area. I made up my bed and rested my large self for a few necessary moments. The structures were tastefully built and adequately designed. Each porch overlooked a beautiful mountain scene. Dr. Trudeau was thoughtful in the positioning and placement of each dwelling. He told me about the idleness that threatened the minds of the children. He even built a small playground for the ones who were not impacted by traditional tuberculosis but had bilious, sanguineous, nervous, or lymphatic cases instead. These folks were mostly still ambulatory and even thirty minutes on the playground kept the children satisfied and amused.

I believed I would enjoy getting to know such a thoughtful man and hoped to become friends with his wife.

I rested my weary body briefly while meals were being prepared. After fifteen minutes or so, I rolled out of bed and walked toward the wafting smell of meatloaf, coming from the kitchen where I willingly offered to help serve the patients. Grateful for the help, the kitchen staff sent me with heaping plates to the circus cottage. The men here were a lively bunch. Seventeen men lined the porch, each with a brightly colored afghan covering his legs and torso. Two men were not seated in lounges, but rather in wheelchairs and they both offered to help me deliver the meals. They balanced plates on their laps and heads as they wheeled and spun about the facility, placing dinners beside each man. One man balanced on the back wheels of his chair, scaring me half to death; he was delighted by my reaction. These men were entertainers. They sat juggling utensils, and pulling doves from beneath their napkins. I would always request this crowd, they were not sullen or desperate, although they coughed and some looked skeletal. They had spunk and that was admirable. I sat with the men as they ate, and listened to their stories about the traveling shows they took part in. One man talked about the tight wire act and how he walked across a wire strung between two buildings ten stories up in the air and survived, only to fall ill with consumption. Another man, who was once the strong man of the show flexed his muscles for me, they were still impressive considering how tiny he had become. One gentleman was the lion trainer, and another in charge of the horses. Several of the men were responsible for setting up the big tents and then taking them down when the show was over. They told me stories late into the evening so that I forgot myself and the dishes that needed washing.

The doctor came to collect me and helped with the return of the dishes, noting who ate what and how much. Charts much like Marjorie's were kept beside each patient and while the doctor was not as personal with them as he was with me, he had an excellent bedside manner and a phenomenal memory.

"Big Joe came here a year ago. I have him on a diet of strictly protein, meat, and eggs, sometimes raw. I thought I was going to lose him in his first month because he was wasting away rapidly. He had no appetite and struggled to breathe, he spit up significant amounts of blood as well. Look at him now, he still coughs, but rarely does he spit up blood. He breathes comfortably and has a great sense of well-being. The mountains provide that, they help enlighten the soul."

"Yes, all the men from the circus seem quite content," I agreed.

"Coerce and cure, that's the methodology. We gather them together within their groups and cure with rest and fresh air, plus diet. They find refinement of the body, ennoblement of the soul, and many find they have heightened artistic talents as well."

"What types of treatments do you administer, Doctor Trudeau?" I asked out of curiosity.

"None. Some doctors believe in bloodletting or purging. Some feel opium provides the best relief, some even suggest smoking, which is preposterous. I believe simply in resting tonics and clean air. Chamomile tea helps the patients rest and relax and so does the environment."

"I'll pray for all the patients tonight, as well as for Collette," I said standing to take my leave.

"I visited her today, while you were dining with the circus men. She is quite a remarkable young lady. She is obviously ill, yet she retains a sense of calm and serenity. She showed me her artwork and I believe that will help keep her occupied and happy. Task work is a very important therapy here. Let's discuss her case more thoroughly tomorrow when I have her specimen back. You should get your rest, you look weary."

"I am tired from the travel, Doctor, that's all."

"Good night then, Christine, and welcome to Saranac Lake."

The following morning I woke to a symphony of birds, forgetting where I was for a moment. There was a brisk chill in the air and I allowed myself a few extra moments in bed. I was tiring more easily now, the baby was bearing down on my bladder and taxing my back.

"Good morning, little one." I spoke quietly to the baby who gave a kick upon feeling my hands on its body.

I was thirty-seven years old, or young, however one looked at it. I was far too old to be with child, and carrying this child was more taxing given my age. Luckily, when I woke, I had numerous things to keep my mind off the pain that started in my lower back and radiated there all day. It was time to be up and about, helping to chart the data for spit specimens as the doctor instructed me.

In the weeks that followed our arrival, I settled into a nice morning routine. I spent the first few hours of my day working on charts, then I visited with Collette. At breakfast time, we chatted over eggs, sausage, and sweetened milk. I used this opportunity to review her charts, which were kept updated by the nurses. On one particular morning, a month after our arrival, the doctor told me that he was pleased with Collette's progress. She was expelling air more freely now than when she first arrived. She didn't have the same blockage that had previously caused her trouble and her coloring was rosier as a result. She was sleeping better and I could tell her appetite was back. Perhaps depression has been setting in back in Skaneateles. It's common among younger patients who are idle for so long. Either way, she was making friends here and getting better. She was delighted to hear there was going to be a co-ed function in one week's time, which she would be permitted to attend.

"Oh, Mother, do you think I might find a boy who likes me?"

"I don't see why not, what's not to like about you? You're beautiful on the inside and out." Collette had wavy, brown hair that hung just below her shoulder blades. Her eyes were a stormy blue with thick curly lashes, and they occasionally turned a deep green color. She had high cheekbones, full lips, and carried herself with excellent posture, shoulders back and down.

I brushed and plaited her thick hair and left her to chat with the other young ladies about the upcoming event.

I crossed paths with the doctor as I walked back to my cottage. "Good day, doctor, I hope my statistical analysis was adequate this morning."

"It always is, and how are you this lovely morning, Christine?" he asked.

"The baby had me up early, but otherwise I slept fine and am ready when you are to discuss how I can help with your new experiment."

"Wonderful, let me finish my notes, and we shall meet back here in an hour."

I wandered around the facilities and listened to the calming sound of a babbling brook. The scent of the balsam, juniper, and white forest pines filled the air. I couldn't help but think about my boys at home in the village of Pittsford, and how much they would have to explore here. I had sent a letter to James with that notion in mind and wondered if there would be work available for him in town.

After discussing the newest experiment Dr. Trudeau wanted to try, I asked him more about the town.

"The town has grown substantially. We had a population of five hundred thirty-three in 1880, but now wealthier sportsmen are taking advantage of the mountain air and moving their entire families here. The village has grown to over one thousand residents. It used to be one had to go to Paul Smith's Hotel in the Adirondack Mountains for a decent meal, but now you can get one here. We have several good restaurants and merchants, as well. What does your husband do?" the doctor asked.

"He's an architect. He has designed homes for many of the wealthy railroad contractors and business owners in Pittsford, and he has even designed parts of the village," I boasted.

"Well, I should think he could find work then if his reputation precedes him."

"Let's hope he is amenable. I can't bear the thought of being away from my baby." I released a sigh, and it didn't go unnoticed.

"Are you afraid of keeping the baby here with you?"

"Why yes, Dr. Kennedy strongly advised against it."

"I see."

"Do you disagree, Doctor Trudeau?" I probed him for his insight.

"No, I don't disagree. It is probably the safest thing for the child, but a child also needs her mother, it's not my place…"

"Well, Collette seems to be doing well here, the staff is wonderful, so I am comfortable leaving to give birth if the local midwife is unable or unwilling to deliver my baby."

"I have not discussed your situation with the midwife yet as I haven't left the facility, but there is an option that came to mind. Little Red, the first cottage I showed you, is vacant. If you want, you could stay there in your own private space and deliver the baby, take care of her for a while and then have your husband take over once the first few vital weeks of life are behind you."

"Oh really, Doctor Trudeau? I should like that very much!" Little Red would be perfect; it was tiny, only fourteen by eighteen feet in size, but it had a wood stove, two cots, a washstand, two chairs, a kerosene lamp, and it's very own front porch, spacious enough for a single chair. Little Blue and Little Green mimicked Little Red architecturally, but I liked where Red was positioned in relation to the other buildings the best.

"It's settled then. I will have it cleaned and prepared for you at once; you have dropped, you know."

I did know my belly was lower now, meaning I had weeks instead of a month and a half until this baby arrived. Several nights after I moved into Little Red, my first contraction came. I woke with a jolt and got out of bed. I placed a shawl around my shoulders and decided to take a walk around the property. When I passed the circus cottage, I ran smack into Big Joe. Big Joe held my arms and paced with me, wearing tread marks in the land. Big Joe had been around the block enough to see that I was in labor; he refused to go to bed while I was in the night air alone. After one exceedingly difficult contraction, I could no longer stand, I asked Big Joe to summon the doctor. I sat on my haunches outside the circus cottage and waited. The stars twinkled brightly, and the frogs croaked in unison, life was all around me now.

"Christine?" Dr. Trudeau called to me, Big Joe trailing behind.

"Over here, doctor." The doctor and two nurses were by my side in mere minutes; Big Joe must have run to him with news of my labor.

"Let's get you to Little Red. How long have you been having contractions?" he asked.

"About an hour, but, doctor, my babies come quickly, I should think the way I feel it will be any moment."

"Can you stand?"

"I don't think so, doctor, I feel I need to push."

The nurses had the foresight to bring blankets; they spread them on the cool ground, and Big Joe brought me a pillow. The doctor lifted my skirts as the nurse held a lantern by my side. The baby was already crowning.

A few circus performers heard I was in labor outside their cottage and came outside to see the spectacle.

"I need to push!"

"Nurse, hold her knees. Okay, Christine, I am going to count to three, push on three."

Big Joe held my hand and I pushed with all my might, screaming and waking even more inhabitants.

"It's a boy!" The doctor brought my son to my chest and cleaned the mess off my legs using the extra towels. He delivered the afterbirth and cut my cord, all by the moonlight and one small lantern. The crease of the morning's first light showed itself as the sun rose over the mountains.

My baby was wrapped in my shawl, and I felt peace and doom all at the same time.

CHAPTER 7

❧

BABY JOE

"I have named the baby Joe," I smiled at Collette. One of the nurses was with him now at Little Red so that I could share the news with my daughter.

I was not physically sore, the experience was quick and relatively painless, similar to my other births. I was lucky that I had wide hips made for birthing.

"Mother, what does he look like? Does he look like you or Father?" Collette beamed as she held my hands.

"He looks like Henry actually. He has a delicate nose and curious eyes and he even has a slight dimple on his left cheek."

"How long will he be here, Mother?" she inquired.

"I will keep him here for a few weeks, I'd like to nurse him that long or more. Then your father will take him to Pittsford and hire a caretaker for him." I began crying at the thought of someone else caring for my baby.

"Mother, don't cry. He will find someone suitable." My daughter had complete faith in her father and I took my cue from her.

"I know he will, it's just I love the infant stage, and the toddler stage, all the stages, really. I just can't bear to part with him." My emotions were getting the best of me as they always did in the days that followed my deliveries.

"Then don't, Mother, let him stay here with you in Little Red," she implored.

"Then I will be of no use to the doctor, and I need to help, I promised to help," I explained.

"Mother, I will be fine here, why don't you and the baby both go home?" she suggested, feeling a pang of guilt at keeping me from my newborn.

"That is out of the question. But I have asked your father to consider moving here. Then I could see you both."

"Have you heard from him?"

"No. I haven't. I wrote to him a week ago, but we are farther away now and it takes longer to deliver the mail."

"I will write to the boys and tell them we have a new baby brother. They will be so happy, won't they?"

"They will, and speaking of Joe, I need to get back to him now."

I was leaking through my dress and needed to nurse immediately. Joe was strong and manly, he didn't have feminine features like James, but had a sturdier jaw and loud cry. He was not a quiet, well-behaved baby, but rather a loud baby who needed attention.

The nurses flocked to him and took turns swaying him and rocking him when he was colicky. Big Joe fashioned a cradle for him out of a drawer and easel, this fit snuggly beside my bed. The staff brought clothing, blankets, and wooden rattles, all which delighted and saddened me. Joe lifted the spirits of everyone on campus, but he would only be here for a little while.

I received a letter from James finally. He was not willing to move the boys here after so much trauma in their lives over the last year or so. He felt they were finally turning a corner and acting like themselves again. He was afraid that moving them would be a setback. They had friends and were doing well in school; they liked the home they rented in the village and were able to walk almost everywhere they went. Their oldest son, Lucas, was reported to have a special lady friend as well.

James had interviewed numerous women for the job of caretaker to Joey and found a young lady by the name of Quinn who met all of his requirements. She had no children of her own so would be able to devote her days to all three of my boys. She was full of energy, was willing to cook, and was very bright and well educated. She was betrothed, but her fiancé passed away from the plague, leaving her alone in Pittsford, searching for work. James planned to arrive within the week to take baby Joey back to Pittsford. He would have him baptized and see to it that he was raised properly.

My heart broke at the thought of missing my baby, but Collette needed me still. It was a sacrifice I had to make.

CHAPTER 8

❦

WINTERTIME

A depression settled into my bones over the desolate and frigid winter months. I stared out my window at the thigh-high snow banks and retreated farther under my bed's coverlet. My baby, Joey, was reportedly doing well while being raised by another woman. His hair was growing in red like his brother Daniel's. I asked for a snippet of his curls for my locket and James obliged me. I carefully tucked the tendrils of hair into my locket and wore it around my neck at all times. I missed having him beside me at night, his little whimpers and moans were soothing. The doctor had allowed me to stay temporarily in Little Red, sensing my distress. But soon I would move back into the staff quarters and once again throw myself into the daily routine of collecting specimens and conducting experiments.

James sent candy and stationery, but no sweet or treasure in the world could replace the weight of my own baby in my arms.

Collette had a marvelous time at the entertainment night months ago listening to musical performances and dancing. She had been showing more spark ever since. She even caught the eye of a young man who began courting her. He sent her books he thought she would like and sent her poetry as well, which helped her escape the winter doldrums. He wrote poems specifically for her with odes to her beauty and talent. She was lovesick. The boy's name was Simon. He was here alone and had lost his entire family to plague years ago, yet he remained upbeat about his circumstances.

Collette wrote in her diary every day and so did her best friend on the grounds, Evelyn. Evelyn's mother, Beverly, also took a job at the sanitarium to help and we became fast friends.

"The girls are certainly paying lots of attention to the boys," Beverly remarked to me one sunshiny afternoon.

"It's about time!" I responded happy to see my daughter behaving like a normal teenager.

"It doesn't worry you?" she asked, concerned.

"Not at all, in fact I have noted a change in Collette since she began her romance with Simon. She is happier now and the doctor said her sputum was clear last week!" I almost didn't want to admit this and jinx Collette, but I was excited at the same time.

"What does that mean? If it is clear, does that mean she is cured?"

"Well no, my understanding is if the culture is clear the bacterium is inactive. All things considered, it's a good sign that means her symptoms are dissipating. I am sure it has nothing to do with Simon really, that's all coincidental, but truly the cool air is helping her. And it will also help Evelyn." I said this confidently, having seen such a drastic change in my daughter.

The winter months were long and daunting, but the frosty air had a way of clearing the lungs. Children and adult patients alike continued to take their cure on the porch even when the weather was at its worst. Everyone simply bundled up tighter, wore more layers, and adapted.

"We've only been here a few months, but I think I see a change in Evelyn, too. The monotony of the routine has had her so bored, but with spring around the corner, she is more eager to face the day and she is coughing less too." Beverly was uplifted by her daughter's progress, as she should have been.

"Wonderful, we should celebrate! Let's go into town this evening and dine out for a change!" I made the suggestion partially to celebrate, but also to get a change of scenery for myself and my friend.

"It's a date!"

"What's a date?" The doctor had come upon us in the lab where we were waiting to learn of his latest experiment on rabbits.

"We've decided to have dinner out tonight. Would you care to join us, Edward?" The doctor had asked both of us to call him Edward, no need for pretenses here.

"Perhaps I will, I could use an evening away. Lottie is in New York and she would be delighted to think of me out from the laboratory for a proper meal."

"It's settled then, at seven o'clock we will depart."

"I can't wait. Now ladies, this week's experiment involves the bunnies before you. I first conducted this experiment in 1885, but need to repeat it to see if my findings remain conclusive." Dr. Trudeau conducted new experiments weekly and we were happy to be a part of them.

In the box there were a dozen rabbits, I picked one up by its thick neck and began to stroke its soft fur while the doctor continued to explain the process.

"We will inoculate five of the rabbits with tubercle bacilli and turn them loose on the island adjacent to us. We will see how they thrive with the sunshine, fresh air, and plenty of food. Similarly, we will inoculate five more, but this time, we will put them in a less than ideal habitat. A damp, dark, confined space without sufficient airflow. The basement is fairly rank, and positively dark and musty, so I thought we would place them there. This way we can determine how the role of environment affects our patients."

"Shall we begin then, Edward?" I asked, ready to get started.

The doctor had previously taught himself how to stain and isolate the bacilli responsible for the disease because it was his fervent hope to discover a cure. He spent most of his afternoons and evenings in his laboratory conducting research. He was a curious man, in spite of all he had been through in his lifetime.

"What about the two remaining bunnies, Edward?" I asked.

"Oh, those are for the children, I thought they might like to have a pet to care for."

"Wonderful, one for the boys and one for the girls, I presume?"

"Precisely. They can take turns feeding the bunnies carrot sticks and celery too."

The doctor believed that caring for an animal, even a bunny, could reduce stress for the children and in some cases, even help them thrive.

During dinner, we asked the doctor about his findings the first time he did the experiment with the rabbits. All but one of the animals he set loose on the island survived and thrived. Conversely, all but one in the basement died of tuberculosis within three months' time. This showed some proof that environments were important. If they could not cure the disease entirely, they could arrest the symptoms and give the patient a more hospitable life.

Dinner was full of laughter. I hadn't laughed in a long while and spent many days lost in thought worrying about Joey and how he was doing. He was four months old now and James indicated he was smiling and had a jolly disposition. His red hair offset his eyes, which were changing from the cloudy blue he was born with to a deep green hue.

I walked toward the girls' cottage and found Collette seated on her cottage steps with Simon, which was permitted according to the rulebook. They held hands and gazed at the stars, pointing out constellations and laughing. I gave them their privacy and met up with several staff members who were discussing plans for another social. The staff thought a dance might be nice for the teenagers, and I volunteered my services to help decorate.

"We could have canning jars with candles, and flowers lining the entryway," I suggested as an economical way to beautify the space for the children.

"Yes, and live musicians, several of the folks in the cottages play instruments and plan to form a band."

And so the next great social event was set into motion. Collette and Evelyn were beside themselves. They were excited to take part in another normal teenage event. Together, with the other girls from their cottage, they decorated a banner for the dance, one they would all sign and treasure.

When the fateful day finally arrived, the girls took their rest for a solid eight hours on the porch. Spring was in the air; the daffodils were budding, snow melting, and birds chirping. It was hard to rest, but they forced themselves to sit still for the afternoon. Afterward they dressed in their finest attire and were escorted to the church where the dance was being held; it was the closest building between the boys' and girls' cottages and had ample space. Music drifted out through the hallways and everyone beamed. Collette and Simon danced, but then he grew winded and needed to sit and rest. Collette seemed to have boundless energy. She looked remarkable as well.

"Your daughter is looking very well, Christine," Edward approached me.

"Yes, she does look well, perhaps it's love?" I suggested.

"It could be, but her specimens have been clear for a month now. I am very encouraged by her waning symptoms. She is more restless too; she wants to be up and about more, which is also good news. The nurses have trouble keeping her at rest for eight hours daily anymore. She wants to walk around the brook and sketch standing on her feet."

"It's so encouraging. At what point can we go home, Edward?"

"That's a difficult thing for me to say. You can leave any time you wish, but my recommendation is that she remains clear for another ten or eleven months before you leave."

"It feels as if it's been forever. Here I mean. We have a new family now, all of you have been so welcoming and kind."

"And you will be irreplaceable, Christine. I mean it."

"Thank you, Edward."

I had been on my feet all week and was feeling a bit exhausted.

"You know, I think I might let Collette have some privacy from her mother's prying eyes. I will see you in the morning."

I took my leave, glancing at my beautiful daughter once more, as she stared into the eyes of her admirer. The dance was a big hit for all. Those who were too spent to dance just enjoyed the music and feast prepared by the kitchen staffers. They had made cupcakes and other sugary sweets, which were only allowed on special occasions.

CHAPTER 9

❧

SPRING AT THE SANS

I woke with a splitting headache. My nose was runny and I felt overheated. I caught sight of a staff member and asked them to relay a message to the doctor that I wasn't feeling well and would stay in bed for the day.

By mid-day, I was coughing and had a fever. I was scheduled to clear the garden today and prepare it for planting but felt like I had the flu. It would be best for everyone if I lay low until it was gone. I wondered who else was sick; perhaps I picked up the germ from dinner last week in town. No matter. I closed my eyes once more and drifted to sleep.

A gentle knock came at my door in the afternoon. Evelyn's mother, Beverly, brought me a bowl of chicken broth. She sat at my bedside while I slurped the salty goodness until I was full. She took my temperature as well. I was at one hundred and two degrees.

"Stay in bed, I will be back this evening with more broth."

I stayed in bed for days, in and out of a feverish delirium. My temperature rose to one hundred and four degrees and the doctor treated me with vapor rubs for my cough and cool cloths for my fever. On my fourth day sick, my cough began to pierce my chest, I was pulling up phlegm, and the doctor asked to examine a specimen. I assured him I was suffering from flu, but told him he could conduct his research if he wished. In the morning, my fever broke but my cough remained persistent and mucus filled my chest cavity. It felt like an elephant was sitting on me.

"Hello Christine, may I come in?" The doctor was back to see me early in the morning of my fifth day being ill. I felt embarrassed by my ghastly appearance but allowed him entry.

"Good morning, Edward, my fever broke during the night. I am certain I will be up and about in a few days' time. How is Collette?"

"Collette is fine, her specimens are clear and she is asking about you."

"Oh dear, I can't see her now and risk her catching my cold. It would take her weeks to recover."

"That's what I told her. But Christine, that's not why I am here. How are you feeling otherwise, are you tired more than usual? Have you been nauseous?"

"Well, no I don't suppose I am. Why do you ask?" I was starting to panic.

"I don't know how to tell you this, but you tested positive for tuberculosis."

"What? That's not possible. Test me again," I begged Doctor Trudeau for a second study.

"I will test you again, you may not have the typical case, but you are positive. I need to discover your origin in order to determine how to help you."

"My origin? Fine then, do an exam, do whatever you must. But I tell you I am just sick with flu."

"You may be sick with flu, but you are also positive for tuberculosis, you could have had it for years but the flu brought it out. I'll gladly test you again, but first, let me examine your lymph nodes, is there pain here?"

He stood behind me and placed his fingers on my neck, working his way from behind my ears all the way down my neck.

"Your glands are rather enlarged, do you feel tenderness?"

"Yes, I do, but doctor, that's normal for a cold or flu."

"Have you had muscle or joint pain?"

"Only since I have been ill, my muscles ache all over. Otherwise, no."

"Okay then, Christine, I will test your specimen once more tomorrow, but at this point I am treating you as a test positive case. You may reside in Little Red, and I will personally see to your care. You are in the best place possible, the air will have you up and around in no time. But you will be treated like a patient, you will be ordered to eight hours a day of porch time, which means no caring for others. Is that clear?"

"Don't tell Collette, I need to do that. Can you please hand me paper and a pen? I need write to James at once." My hands trembled, I was suddenly overwhelmed and unable to control my body. When my children were ill I had the strength to tend them, but being ill myself was not doable. I didn't know how to be cared for and I feared losing James forever now. The tears began and the depression sunk deep into the marrow of my bones.

A gentle knock on my door pulled me from my self-pity and I rose to see who was on my porch. Big Joe stood alone on my doorstep with a large bundle of handpicked flowers.

"For you, my dear, I have heard you were sick with flu and missing little Joe. I hoped these would brighten your spirit."

I brought the bouquet to my nose and inhaled the flowers' sweet scent. This caught me off guard and I started crying once more in front of Big Joe; it was an ugly cry with a heaving chest and snotty nose. Joe handed me his handkerchief with the large embroidered letter "J" and I used it multiple times, finally drying my eyes and calming myself. I folded the hanky in half and then quarters, gripping it tight.

"Sit, sit," Joe admonished me to sit beside him and talk to him about what was troubling me.

"You miss the baby, I can tell. It can't be easy being away from him." Joe thought my upset was entirely due to missing my family.

"Yes, Joe, I do miss my baby, he is growing fat without my milk, but on that from another. I am missing his first smile and his sweet baby smell; that's my favorite part, the way babies smell."

"I know, it's challenging. Have you thought about going home for a while? Collette seems to be doing quite well."

"I can't go home." I started misting again, sobs wracked through my body, and I held Big Joe's hanky to my chest.

Big Joe pulled me to him and held me tight. "There, there, it will be all right, Christine; Collette will understand."

"It's not Collette." I sat speechless in this man's arms for a long moment, enjoying being held and cared for as I haven't in so long.

"What is it then? You can tell me."

"I have tested positive, Joe, and I am terrified now I will never see my boys again." I was nearly cried out, my eyes were swollen, and cheeks blotchy.

"Christine, I am terribly, terribly sorry to hear that. What can I do?" Joe placed a hand on my knee and gave it a squeeze before releasing me from his arms so that we could face one another while we spoke. I told him the doctor's findings and how he planned to retest me the following morning. Collette didn't know yet, no one knew, as a matter of fact. Big Joe promised not to tell anyone the news and I trusted him.

LENA
Spring, 1887

CHAPTER 10

⁂

CHERRY VALLEY

My childhood memories from Middlefield, New York, a small town outside of Cherry Valley, threaten to haunt me now. My father, Villette, passed away following a quick illness when I was only thirteen years old. Until then our existence was meager, but we got by with his field labor and my mother's sewing. Once he passed on, my mother, Mary Goodrich Green, was in a state of shock and we fell short on our mortgage by a few days. The bank, having little compassion for our circumstance, foreclosed on our property, leaving my mother, myself, and my two younger siblings, Grace and Daniel, with no place to call home.

My mother had no time to grieve properly, she was evicted at once, and although we had few belongings, what we had that was worth any money was sold. Our cast iron pots and pans brought money for several days' worth of food, and we took shelter on cots in our church's basement for a couple of nights while creating a plan. We placed an ad on the church bulletin looking for work as seamstresses in exchange for room and board.

It was a difficult time for our family, but we did find work and my mother, Grace, and I set about laundering and mending clothes for the families who showed mercy by having us. My younger brother Daniel often sat within our circle wrapping yarn into tight balls for our evening knitting, otherwise he was able to keep a fairly normal existence. He was too young for farm chores, so he wandered about the homesteads where we earned our keep, playing with the animals and other children residing in the home. Daniel was precious and a tad precocious, earning him favor with the farm wives who gave him extra nibbles and sweets. He grew fat and cheerful, which made me feel resentful on occasion.

My fingers had calluses and fresh blisters from all the sewing; our stitches had to be perfect, nearly invisible, or Mother would make us rip them out and start again. My thimble was too large for my fingers and only got in the way, so I never used it. Mother, Grace, and I took turns laundering and pressing the clothing. Anything that needed mending went into the mending pile for Grace, she did a satisfactory job at patching holes and taking out hems. Mother and I worked with patterns for new shirts and trousers, dresses, smocks, and even coats.

We were usually put up in one room of the home, the four of us shared a bed in the evening, and in the daytime it became our table. We made up the bed, put a flat plank of wood on it, and sketched our patterns carefully on old newspaper. We proceeded to cut out our patterns and then sharpened our scissors before pinning and cutting out material. The first family we stayed with was rather wealthy and they chose silks and velvets for evening dresses. My mother refused to let me cut into the lush fabrics for fear I would ruin them and we'd be sent away. It was imperative we do a good job with our sewing, or we wouldn't get a good recommendation for the next employer. We also had to use our best manners, and help the household in other ways too; often my mother stayed up late doing dishes and scrubbing floors to ensure we would have meals in the coming days.

My mother was a terribly hard worker, but she always managed to make our sewing time fun. She taught my sister and me how to crochet and how to knit complicated patterns such as cables and scallops. She even allowed us to have the sewing scraps, so Grace and I set about making a scrap quilt. Eventually we collected enough scraps that we made a lap quilt for each of us, calico patterns and gingham checks in an array of colors and fabrics were painstakingly pieced together, serving as a reminder of all the places we had worked. The quilt sits on my lap now, warming me, and reminding me to have strength and fortitude in this time of trouble.

My cough started six months ago. It was mild at first and didn't cause much distress initially because I thought it was just an after effect of an intrusive cold. In all my years, I have never had to take any time off from my job at the coffee plant until last week. George, my husband, finally insisted I visit the doctor. The doctor listened to my lungs and paid special attention to my list of symptoms. Once he examined me, he brought George into the tiny room so that we were clustered together. He asked both of us if the children were well, or if any workers at the plant had fallen ill lately.

"Villette, Grace, and Martha are healthy and thriving, doctor. But now that you mention it, Trudy and Spencer were both out last week at the factory. The rumor is they have the plague. I don't work beside them though, and this cough has been going on for months and months."

"Well, my suspicion, Lena, is that you also have tuberculosis or the plague as it's often called." He pushed his glasses higher up on the bridge of his nose as he spoke.

"Doctor, that can't be," George said.

"Wouldn't my children be ill, and my husband? They are all as fit as a fiddle," I implored.

"The disease can lay dormant for years, Lena. It's possible you have been carrying it all this time and the cold brought it forth."

"But, doctor, I feel okay, except for this past week." I sat up straighter in my chair and forced a smile.

"I am willing to keep a sharp eye on you, Lena, but if you start feeling any chest constraint, or start wheezing and coughing blood, then we need to discuss our options."

"I assure you, doctor, I am more than fine. I just need a few good nights of back-to-back sleep. Right, George?"

"Right, Lena." George reached out and grabbed my hand, holding it tight.

"I'd like to see you in the office next week, Lena, I realize you have a work schedule to consider, but I'd be willing to see you after hours on Monday. Say, seven p.m.?"

"Okay, doctor, thank you, I will be here."

That was last Monday. Since then, I have begun to spit up blood mixed with mucus and feel that I have the flu all the time. My muscles ache and my body feels heavy all over. My birds know something is wrong because I haven't been up and about to offer them treats or perch them on my shoulder lately. I have six parakeets, four of which are males. Luckily, the two females get along or we'd have trouble. The females are green breasted with pink faces and have a high-pitched singing voice. Many people find it fascinating that parakeets can sing; it's not quite as pretty as a canary's song, but they sound lovely to me. I can tell they are sleeping now, not only because of the way their heads are nestled tightly into their breasts, but also because of how fluffy they appear. When they are napping, they fluff their feathers to trap the warm air around them and make themselves cozy. When my girls are awake, they chew on toys and cuttlebone as if they were nesting. My girls keep themselves clean with regular preening and interestingly, they take turns feeding one another seeds that have been regurgitated. The cage is beside me now as I sit and fondle the scrap quilt; the worn velvet patch has felt my worries over the years as I rub it and think.

My children need their mother. However, I have already lost one baby and don't want to risk getting the others sick. My Eva Eliza was a "blue baby" and the pain was unbearable. The thought of losing another child, particularly to this disease, is unfathomable.

"We will use extreme caution, Lena. I will do the cooking and the dishes and you can take your meals apart from us if it makes you feel better," my husband George said to me.

"What if they already have it? What if it's just dormant like mine was?"

"Well, that may be the case, but I am willing to take extra measures for them, and for you." George reassured me, and I thanked God for giving me such a remarkable husband.

"Maybe we should boil water and pour it over the dishes? The heat would kill anything, wouldn't it?" I wondered aloud.

"It can't hurt." So every night after the family ate; my husband scrubbed the dishes with soap and then laid them in the sink so that he could rinse them with boiling water. Sometimes he did this twice, his obsessive nature exposing itself.

My illness prevented me from working at the factory any longer. I spent my time at home now and did lots of sewing and mending while the children were at school. I spent most of my time in my room with the blue parakeets, my two oldest males, named Vern and Pete, to keep me company. Occasionally I spent time on the small porch that overlooked the street, allowing me to see into the neighbors' lives. This is where Rascal and Denny were housed. No one else on the street was ill, and although some asked why I was home, we didn't tell them it was due to consumption right away.

After a few months, I became bedridden. My cough intensified, and my entire body felt weak from head to toe. I needed help going to the backhouse and dressing was a difficult task. Making tea for myself was tiresome, and George was becoming overwhelmed.

The parakeets were flustered and could sense something was amiss. They hadn't been outside of their cages for weeks, the children were too busy to play with them, and I just wasn't myself.

The doctor suggested we look into a sanitarium, or cure cottage, nearby that could provide me with better care. The advantage would be closer monitoring of my symptoms and a better environment for my children who tiptoed around me now. They feared waking me, or disturbing me, and furthermore, they feared becoming like me.

We were not a family with great means; we worked long, arduous hours to pay our bills, and we also tithed ten percent of our wages to the church. At the end of the month, if any money was left we put in a preserve jar that was hidden in our closet behind the two pairs of shoes we owned.

Our initial inquiry was to a sanitarium in Schenectady. They had beds available but I needed to pay a monthly sum for my room and board, or have a family member come to help with my care. Neither of these options would work for us.

The days ticked by, the children would be enjoying their summer recess soon and I desperately wanted to finish the afghan I was working on for Grace. She made a request before I fell ill for her very own afghan, made with Granny squares in vivid colors. My fingers ached and became stiff, but the small squares were piling up beside me. I only had twenty-four more to make before assembling the squares together. Grace begged to help me; she loved making granny squares and was good at it too. Of all my children, she had a knack for sewing, like her namesake, my sister.

After our days moving from farm to farm with my mother, my sister became a master dressmaker and seamstress. Her tatting and smocking was the best I had ever seen and I admit I was jealous. Her hem lines were perfectly straight, her stitches never lazy, and when she fell in love and was set to marry a farmer, she made her very own wedding dress with a bustle. It was the only impractical thing she had ever done with her savings, but she wanted a wedding gown, so she used her money to buy scraps of lace and bolts of ivory satin from the sale bin. She even went so far as to add a few hand-sewn pearls along her wrists' cuffs. She kept the dress in a closet with mothballs, and was saving it for her own daughters to wear someday.

I didn't allow Grace to come in my room and sit by my side and crochet, but she often came to my doorway and peeked in at my progress. My pace had slowed, and now it was taking me the better part of a week to make one six-inch square. My needles fumbled in my trembling hands and more than once I dropped them entirely in a coughing fit.

I slept alone now; George was on the couch, because my coughing kept him up at night and made his work shift difficult. I always cracked a window because I found the crisp air to be helpful when I felt like I was drowning in my own mucus. I was coughing up more blood now as well and felt like my days were numbered. How did people survive this disease? I would rather stay in my own home and be among my family in my dying days than be sent away.

"Dear, you are getting worse, we have to get you better care." George said to me one night after coming into the room and finding me looking rather gaunt.

"I'd rather be here, with you, and I can't bear to be away from the children."

"I know, Lena, but it's best for you and them; they need you and you could be cured. There are other sanitariums; in fact, there is one in the Adirondacks that the doctor has written to."

"I didn't ask him to do that!" I was fuming mad, no one understood that leaving my children and my parakeets would be a death in and of itself.

"He really thinks your particular case is milder than some others he has seen; therefore, if you are willing to try the porch cure the sanitariums offer, you just might feel better."

"I can't. I can't bear it, George."

"Lena, I know. But the children have me and each other. Villette will help me with the household chores and Martha and Grace can help with the cooking and cleaning. We will be fine."

"But I would miss you something awful."

"We will write regularly, and pray nightly."

"George, do you really think I could get better?"

"I do. From what the doctor has shared with me, other patients with far worse symptoms have had success in the mountains. He thinks it's the crisp air and the lifestyle, along with the diet, which is specific for anyone with consumption."

"Okay, have the doctor send the letter."

"He already has. I will stop by tomorrow on the way to work to see if he's had word back yet."

I had difficulty sleeping that night. I wasn't a warm, cuddly, demonstrative mother, but I always wanted to be near my children. I worried over them something fierce and the thought of not being here during their formative years made me depressed. A deep, numbing sensation settled into my bones, my arms grew heavy with grief. I agreed to go away, but for how long was a question no one could answer. There was no cure for the plague, only ways to help your symptoms and improve the quality of life. But my quality of life would diminish once I left my family so, either way, I didn't win.

CHAPTER 11

❧

SUMMER AT THE SANS

Dr. Trudeau welcomed me to the Saranac Lake sanitarium in the Adirondack Mountains with a balsam pillow and a rulebook. It was a brilliant set up. However, I immediately grew shy and nervous by the sheer number of people taking their rest side by side outdoors. I didn't have many friends at home. I chose to keep mostly to myself. I worked and spent my time with my family, and while I had neighbors to pass time with, I usually busied myself with tasks indoors.

The doctor insisted on using a wheelchair to show me around. He wheeled me through a corridor at the main facility, which led to a porch lined with beds. The bed I was assigned was tucked in the farthest corner. A chart with my name, Lena Green Thompson, hung from its post. I was to take my rest here among all the other female patients. In the evenings, I would reside with a lady named Rhonda, who I had yet to meet. Her portion of our room was tidy enough and I noted her basket of yarns, so I assumed we would get along fine and could maybe teach each other a thing or two. We both had bedside tables; hers held a photograph of a man, a sputum cup, nasal douche, and a stack of postcards. Later, when I unpacked, I would place the picture of my family on my lace doily at the corner of the table nearest me.

My day was planned out before me. Patients were to rise at six-thirty in the morning and breakfast was served precisely at seven o'clock. After dishes were cleared, sputums were collected, then vitals were taken and registered. Rest time was scheduled between ten a.m. and noon followed once more by vitals. Then the main meal of the day was served and it usually consisted of a large portion of beef, pork, or chicken, and some steamed greens. We weren't allowed to use salt or butter for flavorings and I grew used to appreciating the food as it came straight from the garden to table. Following the dinner, patients were once again required to rest or permitted to do task work. For now, I was required to rest all day, until my symptoms abated.

The doctor didn't tolerate any negative energy, so the ladies did their best to put on a happy face and take part in the activities that were held. I chose to close my eyes and pretend I was asleep most afternoons on the porch. I didn't like the proximity of other ladies to me, I was private and this was not a private institution. My bodily fluids were measured and recorded, my sputum was collected and tested each morning. Even my meals were monitored. I was prevented from eating anything sweet, and only allowed beef, eggs, and dairy initially.

I missed my family something terrible and could not disguise my anguish.

The cool mountain air did appease my lungs, I admit. I coughed in fits, but the blood and feeling of drowning abated as the time went on. I grew restless by my fourth week. While I overlooked a mountain stream and the scenery was lovely, boredom had taken over. I wrote to my family daily and started reading from the book carts that were rotated among living quarters.

I asked for George to send me more yarn; I needed ten skeins for a proper-sized lap blanket and decided I might as well make a few while I was taking my rest on the porch.

The lady to my left was named Eleanor, and she was in her early twenties; she too had children at home. One afternoon she began a soft whimper into her handkerchief. She didn't want anyone to hear so she stifled her sobs. I pulled my slippers up and over my heels and got out from my bed to offer her much-needed comfort.

"There, there, Eleanor, what's bothering you?" I pulled her blanket tighter around her to keep her warm. It had been snowing heavily and the frosty air was brisk. We all wore gloves and hats to keep our extremities warm, but sometimes the cold was bone chilling and Eleanor was shivering.

"My children, they are growing up without me, my husband writes that my oldest girl just lost her first tooth, and that my son is learning his letters," she continued to sob.

"I have children at home as well, it's difficult, I know. I wonder every second of every day what they are doing and how they are faring. But I have to put my trust in my husband and God that they will be taken care of." I adjusted Eleanor's pillow and noted that she didn't have any books beside her.

"Eleanor, would you like to borrow one of my books? It might keep your mind off your children."

Eleanor began crying even more now. "I can't read, Lena, I can't read."

"Oh. I suppose I could teach you if you'd like."

"I would like that, but I would prefer to learn to knit and crochet like you do."

That is how I began giving lessons at the sanitarium for sewing, knitting, and crocheting. I taught all levels and found that it was most enjoyable, I would even claim some of the women I taught were becoming my friends. One woman in particular was to my liking. Her name was Christine.

Christine joined our Thursday evening knitting club and was adept at learning more complicated patterns. She had nimble fingers and was able to hold her needles in such a way that she completed her rows with few mistakes and in a timely fashion. She was making an afghan for her friend Joe from the circus quarters. The colors she chose were vivid and bright, like he was, according to her.

"Perhaps we can sell blankets as a means to obtain more funds for the Sans," Christine said to me during one of our club meetings. She was tying off her ends as she spoke. "Then even more people can come here for help. Right now the doctor tells me they can't build a new building until they have raised five hundred dollars."

"Goodness, that's a lot of money. I don't think we can sell five hundred dollars' worth of blankets, do you?" I asked sincerely.

"Well, no, I don't think we can do it with blankets alone, but I was talking with Big Joe and he and the gentleman from the circus quarters are planning on building boats this winter. They already have the wood chopped and the boats measured out."

"Grand, I had no idea!" I said, nodding Christine to go on.

"The children have been making pottery and are willing to hold a sale, and the Cuban gentlemen have been making brass sculptures, they really are quite lovely. Juan came by to show me one he made of a swan. He hammered the wings so they catch the light, marvelous really."

"I'd like to see that; goodness, how many clubs do you suppose we have here that meet on Thursday nights?"

"At least a dozen or so." One of the other women chimed in.

"A dozen, indeed, I should like to try my hand at something new. What types of things do they make?" I asked, directing my question to Christine because she seemed to know the most.

"Well, some of the clubs simply meet to discuss books and poetry, other clubs meet to sing songs and play their instruments. Others give instruction in arts and crafts. Besides us and the potters, there are the woodworkers, painters, shoemakers, and like I said, the sculptors."

"I don't suppose we could encourage each group to donate several of their pieces of art for a sale do you?"

"It doesn't hurt to ask! Joe already offered one of the boats to such a cause. I don't know why we couldn't have a sale in town. Perhaps Dr. and Mrs. Trudeau would be willing to set up a booth and handle the exchange of money."

"I wish I could go to town, I miss seeing people going about their business." This was odd coming from me, seeing as I was more introverted than extroverted, but being isolated in the woods makes one yearn for activity.

"Perhaps we can, perhaps we can make an event out of it!" Christine finished the row she was working on and pushed her yarn to the tops of her needles. She settled them on her lap and looked outward toward the edge of the property. She was deep in concentrated thought when a smile pursed her lips.

"What are you thinking, Christine?" Betsy, one of the other ladies, asked.

"I was thinking we all need a festival."

CHAPTER 12

✻

FESTIVAL PREPARATIONS

People from different cottages and buildings came together to help plan and coordinate the upcoming Winter Festival. Everyone wanted to be involved, even the children volunteered their time and voiced their ideas and opinions.

Our first meeting was led by Dr. Trudeau and his wife, Lottie. They relied heavily on donations to pay their staff and buy supplies, so in addition to raising money for a new building, they hoped the festival would provide extra funds for medicinal supplies and food.

It was agreed that the festival would primarily be to raise funds, but that in addition to booths selling our wares, we would hold activities that would attract the family members of the Sans patients as well as the folks from town.

The ice-encrusted lakes beckoned skaters to glide across their glassy surface, and the fluffy snow atop the hilly peaks had children and adults alike clamoring to sled and ski. We would charge a dime per ride and offer hot chocolate for a nickel. There was even talk of snow sculpture competitions; teams would pay a small fee to enter the competition, and the winners would take a cut.

Christine and Big Joe offered to co-chair the event. They assigned each group of craft people with a task; the artists were to design posters for the event, and the sculptors were given the task of setting up the tents and tables. The circus men were going to entertain the crowd with juggling acts and stilt walking; Big Joe would pick up his weights once more and act as the strong man, while several other circus performers would dress as clowns and add merriment to the event just by being present. The children would set up a table for face painting and come up with designs such as butterflies and roses that they could easily replicate on cheeks. Some folks wanted the task of cooking, and planned to make hot soups and fresh breads, plus sweets of all kinds. Others created a group of tenors who would perform. The doctor and volunteers offered to hang posters in town and spread the word at the local library and church. The shoe factory workers offered to be on clean up detail.

We all wrote to our families at once describing the activities and events that would take place. Having an engagement such as this on the calendar made us all giddy with joy.

As the date for our festival approached, the sweet sound of strings could be heard echoing all across the mountains. The musicians were practicing their acts, which included singing and dancing, a recitation contest, and even humorous drama. A group of musicians formed during this time and hence became known as the "festival group." The festival group was comprised of a piano player, a violinist, a flutist, and several singers. More and more individuals joined the choir that was started, and more often, our Thursday evening clubs were entertained by their melodies and voices.

Christine didn't show up to several of our club nights during this time because she and Big Joe were working on the business end of things. They created a budget and were working on setting a fundraising goal so large it would build not one, but two new facilities.

I wrote to my husband and children right away, asking them to circle the date of February sixteenth on the calendar. I realized our funds were very limited but prayed they could find a way to journey to the Adirondacks to visit me during this time. George would have to put in for the time off now, and the children would have to arrange the short vacation with their teacher. A week passed before a letter addressed to me arrived; my family was planning to come to the festival and stay for three days' time.

My heart exploded with gratitude; I don't know how George could afford this trip, but it would be among the greatest gifts he ever gave me. I missed my family something fierce. I was coming out of my shell, had made friends with Eleanor and Christine, and did enjoy teaching, that much was true. But nothing and no one could take the place of my beloved family. I thought of them every second of every day, wondering what the children were learning, how their days had gone, how work was for George, what foods they were preparing in my absence.

I also missed the constant chatter of my birds; they were indispensable to me, and my heart broke when I thought of them.

The pain of missing them did ease with time, but it never went away. My lungs felt better because of the balsam pillow I slept with and the cool, crisp mountain air. I didn't hack up blood the way I used to and could now walk without feeling compromised and short of breath. The cold cure indeed worked for me, but I still wished and longed for home. My specimens showed signs of active consumption, so I would be here for a while, but I dreamed of my homecoming. I dreamed of my darling daughters' weddings and being present at the birth of my grandchildren. I even dreamed of George, being swept up in his embrace once more, feeling his soft, sweet kiss upon my lips, and feeling the beating of his heart as I lay down night after night upon his chest.

Christine was not so lucky. Her husband had the means to attend the festival but flat out refused to bring the children anywhere close to those of us with plague. Christine said she understood; she had lost two children to the disease and her husband was being protective.

She came to one of our Thursday evening clubs with swollen eyes and tear-stained cheeks, but proceeded to discuss the event as if nothing were amiss with her. Collette joined us on occasion now too; she was a lovely girl, a love-struck girl who was growing into a true beauty. Her beau, Simon, was not faring so well. She wheeled him to his club with the sculptors on one evening, but when she left early to go pick him up and wheel him to his home he was not there. He had a coughing fit so substantial the doctor was summoned and was with him throughout the night. Simon was failing when so many of us were thriving.

I found Christine the following morning, weeping softly into her hands, by the creek that wound around our building.

"What is it, Christine?" I asked gently as I approached her from behind, the trickling water's soothing sound not far off in the distance.

"It's just not fair," she continued to cry. "Simon, he is so young and optimistic, I am just so afraid for him."

"And for Collette," I added.

"Yes, she loves him, and I can read the pain on her face that his demise is causing her."

"I bet she feels guilty because she is doing so well these days, and yet he seems to be getting worse." When the ladies were discussing the young folks at one of our club meetings, Simon's name came up because there was growing concern for him. No one ever visited him or sent letters, he only had Collette and she cared for him as if they were wed.

"Young love, so pure and innocent." I remarked, thinking of the lovers sneaking out for a kiss under the moon, or holding hands when they thought no one was watching.

"That's why it isn't fair, none of this." My friend gestured to the land and buildings around her, before erecting her posture and deeply inhaling the cool air. She would start to hyperventilate if she were unable to calm herself. I kneaded her neck and shoulders and then we sat in silence on a log, contemplating our lives with each inhalation, expressing our sorrow with each exhalation.

"What can I do?" I asked Christine.

"What can any of us do?" she answered.

"I suppose all any of us can do is be there for your daughter to offer support. Please tell her if she needs anything at all to come to me."

"I will, Lena, and thank you."

I turned away from the creek bed and walked to my resting chair, settled myself underneath my coverlets, and began to nod off. I dreamed once more of my own children and awoke to a hysterical scene. People were carrying on and crying into their hankies all around me, Nurses, staff members, and patients alike were upset, it seems as if someone had passed away during the night hours. That someone was Simon. Everyone was sad when a patient died, but especially when it was a child. The irony is that he had already died when Christine and I were discussing him; perhaps we both had a sense of his doom. I immediately thought of Collette and said a long, heartfelt prayer on her behalf.

Simon's burial was scheduled to take place the following afternoon. Collette never left his side except to seek my help in finishing her lap blanket for him; she wanted him to be buried with a piece of her. I picked up her stitches where she left off and went swiftly to work. Knit, purl, knit, and purl. Collette sat stoically as people came to pay their respects, she never dropped one tear while the minister spoke of her beloved. It was only when she placed the finished blanket across Simon's spindly legs that she began to shudder. Her mother, Big Joe, and I were all beside her at that point and together we carried her away from Simon, to her own lonely bed.

Collette's loss became Christine's undoing. My once confident, strong, optimistic friend became sullen and quiet. Even talk of the upcoming festival did little to revive her spirits. I tried pulling her back to us by asking about the fundraising efforts or questioning after Collette's health.

It turned out Collette had been free from bacilli in her sputum for over six months now. Soon she could be released out into the world without a care or concern. Yet, this beautiful young lady, who had experienced her first true love while here, seemed far older than her years.

Collette's condition was cause for celebration, I would give anything to be healthy and released so that I could go on living, truly living, with my family. Yet the two women sat side by side in silence on the porch that overlooked the pristine mountain caps that jutted themselves against the sky, not alone, but lonelier than they had ever felt before.

I slipped into my own depression during this time when news from home arrived in the form of a letter. My husband was not granted time off from work. Too many people had fallen ill at the factory, and they could not release him or his job would be in jeopardy. I would not see my children, feel their embrace, or hear their laughter. I would be alone once more, but I was damned if I would wallow. I would get better and go home to them if it was the last thing I ever did.

BIG JOE

CHAPTER 13

❧

AUTUMN

I worked alongside Harry and Benny for two months. The guide boat was almost complete now. I had one more coat of varnish to apply and then it would be put up for auction at the winter festival, our first large event to raise funds for the Sans. The boat was looking good and I'd be surprised if she didn't fetch fifty dollars. She was designed to carry three men, or a maximum of six hundred pounds. She'd ride smoothly across the water, barely leaving ripples in her wake. I'd like to take her out for her maiden voyage if possible, before the snow starts to fall again and the waters freeze up at the river's edges.

The festival had been set into motion by my friend, Christine, a genuinely kind woman who was ahead of her time when it came to business. She had a head for arithmetic and business like no other woman I knew, except for Donna. I dipped my rag into the varnish bucket and thought back to when I first met Donna a lifetime ago.

Donna was among the group of women who made up the ringmaster's posse. She had an ample bosom that spilled out from whatever dress she was wearing. Her hair was red and curly, making me wonder if her woman's curly cues were also red. I spent way too much time thinking about Donna. I came upon her on more than one occasion when the ringmaster was nuzzling her bosom with his face, or cupping her from behind with his dirty hands.

She caught me watching the exchange on one such occasion and I could feel the deep blush rush to my cheeks, not because I was embarrassed for her, but rather for myself. I had never even seen bosoms like Donna's, let alone touched them. I dreamed about Donna and what it would be like to have a woman who was so willing. Donna was off limits, of course. I was just a measly hand that set up and took down the tents.

The job wasn't difficult, but the pay was lousy. I did get free room and board albeit the only place for me to lay my head at night was with the entire trapeze team and contortionists in one boxcar. The team contorted their bodies every which way and somehow managed to fit themselves, all twenty-six of them, in one car. I was number twenty-seven and slept on top of a supply crate. Several of the team were coupled off and made loud uncomfortable noises; they used curtains to partition off private space for themselves, but all the grunting and groaning couldn't be masked. I closed my eyes in deep concentration, thinking of Donna and somehow, somewhere during the night, things finally grew quiet and all around me were the whistles and even sounds of breathing and farting that soothed me to sleep.

I owe a debt of gratitude to the ringmaster for putting me with the trapeze artists; if I hadn't had my experience sleeping with such a large crowd I doubt I could get my rest here at the Sans. There were more than seventeen of us circus performers in my large building, some of whom were with me at Barnum and Bailey, but others were from Ringling and smaller traveling shows. We all had individual acts to stake a claim on and differentiate ourselves with but other than that, it seemed we show folk had a similar outlook on life. There wasn't one among our bunch who was sour. Everyone was bright and cheerful, regardless of our circumstances.

In all my years around the circus, I only saw one person cry and that was Donna. I came upon her with the animals. I had taken over Simms' job that day feeding the animals, he wasn't feeling well and I had seen him at task enough times that I felt confident I could handle the job as a favor to him. I couldn't have been more wrong. The horses brayed nervously when I approached with their oats, they clomped at the ground and whinnied at me. Rather than collect myself, I just threw the whole pail over their stall and hoped the large beasts could find the oats between their hay and get enough to eat. The tigers had no teeth, but were still a force in and of themselves. The female was named Shirley, which I always thought was funny. Who in the world decided to name this fierce creature Shirley? Shirley growled at me and I was terrified to lift her chute and slide the raw meat mixture underneath. I held my breath and counted to three before summoning the courage to do this in one fell swoop.

I thought I heard a rustle in the hay pile beside me and figured rats were running about. But when the rustle turned to laughter, I knew immediately it was Donna.

"I feel better now," she said to me, but her tear-stained cheeks and red-rimmed eyes told a different story.

"Golly, I didn't know anyone was there. Pardon me, ma'am," I said, tipping my cap to the lady who had crawled out from the hay and now stood before me.

"That was quite a show you just put on. You shouldn't close your eyes when reaching into the tiger's cage, you know that, don't you?" she asked. Seeing her up close I realized she had delicate features and green eyes. She was freckled and sturdier than I thought.

"Well, I don't ordinarily feed the animals and I am embarrassed to admit it, but they frighten the hell out of me." I laughed at myself and Donna laughed with me.

"Let me help you." Donna led the way from the tigers to the lions, reaching into the slop bucket that held their food.

"You do know they get fed any dead animals we come across during our travels, don't you?"

"Whhat?" I stammered.

"Did you see the horse on the side of the road that we passed yesterday on the way to Endicott?"

"Why, yes, I did. Poor creature."

"Poor creature indeed, he's now this here fella's dinner." Donna quickly and expertly lifted the latch on the side of the lion's cage and slid in the tray holding the dead horsemeat. My eyeballs were bulging out of my head and Donna gave a laugh.

"You're funny, how come I haven't noticed you before?" she asked.

"Well, ma'am, I don't know, but I sure have noticed you." The words were out of my mouth and I wanted to punch myself for being so stupid. She belonged to the ringmaster; it was clear that no one was to mingle with his woman, no one. We marched on to the cramped cage that held the black bear. Once more, Donna filled a tray with slop from the bucket and expertly slid it into the animal's cage.

"Have you helped Simms before?" I asked, curious how she was so at ease with the animals.

I noticed Donna had a stretch of several long thin bruises running across her neck. I reached out to trace them, but she pulled away. Her eyes welled with tears and she stood against the framework of the trains that housed several of the animals, silently letting herself weep.

"What's wrong, ma'am? Is someone hurting you?" I asked, certain it was the ringmaster.

"It's no bother, you should run along and finish with the animals. I have to go pretty myself up anyway for the show tonight."

"Don't go," I told Donna and tried to grab for her.

She called back that I better watch myself with the elephants, they could stomp me. Then she was gone, as suddenly as she had appeared, she disappeared. I was left to feed the elephants, but they were easier, I could throw heads of lettuce and apples into their boxcar and be done. It was the snakes, which I intentionally left for the end, that scared me the most. Snakes only ate live food; I found a few rats in a bucket, left for Simms to slip into the snakes' cage. I assumed incorrectly they were both for the large boa that was staring me down as I approached. I grabbed a rat by its tail in my right hand and with my left, I unhinged the lock and began to open the door. I had the door open a few inches when I felt fangs clamp down on the tendon between my thumb and forefinger. I frantically shook the second snake, which was attached to my hand, and hit it against the cage repeatedly in an attempt to release it. It was a smaller, meaner animal that finally let go of my hand, right before I fainted. When I came to, Donna was standing over me pressing a cool cloth to my forehead.

"I heard you scream. You've been bitten by the baby rattlesnake; the doctor is here to take a look at you."

The snake charmer sat in the corner, swaying from side to side, hypnotizing me into slumber. When I woke once more, my arm was swollen to twice its size and the ringmaster was beside me.

"The doctor says he has no medicine for you, we have never had a snake bite before on the show. You are the first," he stated as a matter of fact.

"So I might die?" I asked, frantic.

"You might, but you also might live. Donna will tend to you and the doctor will check on you every day." The ringmaster was loud and had an authoritative air that was not to be questioned. I believe I had inconvenienced him with my bite and swollen arm.

My throat hurt and Donna tried to get me to take small sips of water, but instead I nodded in and out of consciousness once more, the pain from my bite unbearable.

Someone was stroking my feet, rubbing the flat bottoms in a way that took away my pain. I opened my eyes and saw a Chinese woman manipulating my toes and the tendons between them. Whatever method she used, it worked. My pain diminished when she applied pressure to my middle toe and heel simultaneously. She kneaded the palms of my hands, as well. The woman came three times daily and by the second day, I noticed my swelling was going down. By the end of the week, I realized I would survive the bite, but only because of this woman, not Donna who no longer showed up to care for me. The Chinese woman bathed me and brushed my hair; she fed me a salty broth and spoke to me in a language I could not understand, yet I understood her intention was to get me well.

When I was finally up and around, I ran directly into Donna who had a fresh welt across her cheek.

"Who did this to you?" I asked.

"I fell," she replied.

"I will find out who is smacking you around and you can be sure whoever it is won't like answering to me."

I was twenty-two years old, had never been with a woman, but I had seen a man strike a woman many times in my life, in my own home. It angered me and it was the reason I left when I did. My father struck my mother so many times she barely ever spoke, she flinched in my father's presence and the few times I tried to intervene she was harmed even more. My father was a farmer and a drunk. My mother was a lowly wife with no education and means. Her only job was to help on the farm by preparing the food and feeding the animals. If my father didn't like a meal, he'd throw the plate on the floor and make my mother eat the droppings like a dog. He would hold her down, her nose to the splintering wood, his fingers leaving marks on her neck. If she cried there would be more, if she obeyed she would eventually be let up and permitted to cook another meal. One time, I saw my mother hack into my father's stew. It was our secret.

I despised men who used their brawn against women. Someone, and I knew just who, was doing this now to Donna. Donna refused to admit she was being beaten, but more and more often, she had makeup on from sunup to sundown, her face contorted beneath all the thick creamy makeup she used to hide the purple-green bruises. I took to spying on the couple and found it wasn't only the ringmaster who hit Donna but his strongman as well.

I decided that if I became a strongman I could protect Donna. I began lifting weights with Bruno, the current strongman. I began doing chin ups and pushups. I did a series of abdominal exercises each night that entertained the trapeze troops who counted out loud with me until I reached two hundred. I began lifting the trapeze artists themselves. I would lie on the solid floor and gather them in my hands, benching them like a weight. The grace they exhibited naturally along with their extreme ability to remain still made this exercise possible. They had perfect precision as well and could mount into my arms and dismount when I was done with very little effort. Before too long, I was able to lift the man in the group that I estimated weighed a solid one hundred fifty pounds. He was more difficult on account of his thick muscles, so I began rolling the tree trunks the elephants gnawed on. I lifted them up and dropped them down, repeating the process across the lands we had staked to set up our acts.

As I worked on my strength, I got stares from various performers. The midgets often climbed across my back when I did pushups; the fat woman sat on my ankles and shins, nearly crushing me to death while I tried to get across the fields with her dragging me down, creating a resistance.

The bearded woman just sat eating her dumplings while she cheered me on. Yet other performers wondered at my reasoning. I was only a tent man; I simply set up and took down the tents. All the other tent men spent their days drinking and screwing. I was different. I wanted more.

The man who trained the costumed poodles approached me one afternoon; he sidled up to me and said, "You have an audience."

Indeed, the ringmaster was watching me as I worked to become the new strongman. One afternoon he approached me, asking how much I weighed and what kind of tricks I could do. I didn't have any tricks. I told him I was just keeping my body fit.

"Learn some tricks," he said, "and you can go on stage with the strongman." He blew his cigar's smoke in my face as he left.

"What kind of tricks do you suppose I should learn?" I asked Donna when I ran into her again after breakfast.

"Can you break open a watermelon with your head?" she asked.

"Or how about this, can you pull a boxcar?" she wondered out loud.

I knew I couldn't pull a boxcar but I would try to crush a watermelon. I was successful. The watermelon crushing became my first side act; people clapped loudly when I bashed it against my head, sending the black teardrop-shaped seeds scattering across the floor. Although I often saw stars after my first act, it was my second that was death defying. The ringmaster devised an act he thought certain I could accomplish. He refused to tell me what it entailed, he would rather show me, he said, at our next stop.

So it was in Pennsylvania that I was chained to a chair, hands behind my back. Nothing but sheer strength could set me free. But the ringmaster wasn't done; he decided to let the tigers in on the act. Shirley was circling me as I tried ferociously to break free from my chains. I was less worried about Shirley than I was about her male counterpart. I knew he had at least a few of his canines because I could see them as he stalked me like prey in the wild. He circled me twice and then sauntered off to get into a crouched position. His eyes never left mine. I fumbled with the chains, using all my strength to break them apart, to no avail. But when the cat leapt toward me, and I was fighting for my life, I used my oblique muscles as well as my arms and burst free from the chains that bound me. I leapt from the stage to an applause so great even the ringmaster was surprised. He patted me on the back and said, "I knew you could do it, son. What did you say your name was?"

"Strongman, just call me Strongman."

So forever more I became the Strongman; the original was waning in his enthusiasm for the circuit. He was growing fat around his middle, although he could still bend steel, which was impressive to me, he had few other people who found this so. When compared to my feats, he had little to stand on. He was demoted to tent duty, and I was promoted to head Strongman and bodyguard to Donna.

CHAPTER 14

❧

CIRCUS DAYS

Donna convinced the ringmaster that I deserved my own place to sleep. After all, I was bringing in most of the crowd now. She also ordered the cook to give me at least half a dozen eggs each morning, along with my own loaf of bread. I ate greedily and grew to over six feet and five inches tall. I was thick and muscular, and now the act involved three chains instead of just one when facing the big cats.

Donna found me a boxcar that held supplies and helped me set up a corner with fresh hay where I could sleep. Only the first night I lay down, she didn't leave. She watched me undress and undressed herself right before my eyes.

I gulped and stammered as I spoke. "Wwwhat are you doing?" I asked.

"What does it look like I am doing, Strongman? I am giving you what you've always wanted." She climbed on top of me and gave me what I never knew I was missing.

I became obsessed with Donna; she was everything to me. We made love nearly every night, exploring new tactics and positions, and ways to please one another.

"Doesn't the ringmaster want you with him?" I asked cautiously one night.

"He is otherwise occupied right now," she stated.

"Does that make you jealous? He's with one of your friends?"

"First off, they ain't my friends and second, I would hardly call Benny someone I should be jealous over."

"Benny, as in Benny the unicyclist? That Benny?" I asked, unable to hide my surprise.

"Yes, that Benny. He calls me to bed, and feigns sleep and as soon as I get up to go back to my room, I see Benny sneaking in."

"Jeepers. I don't know what else to say."

"It gives us more time to be together so I am happy. Strongman, what's your real name?" Donna asked. I was afraid if she knew my name she'd no longer be enamored with me for who she thought I was. I decided to trust in her and told her at last. "My name is Jeremy. Jeremy Smith."

She repeated my name as she swirled my chest hairs between her fingers. My name rolled off her tongue in three long syllables. Before she could finish I captured her and brought her to my mouth, kissing her with renewed passion. Our secret affair went on for nearly a year, no one was the wiser, and everyone was content. She went to the ringmaster when she was called, but that was a rare. The ringmaster had new love interests and furthermore wanted to pawn Donna off on some of his wealthy friends. I hated this notion, the ringmaster expected Donna to sleep with any man who was willing to pay. He was turning her into a prostitute and neither of us liked it.

"What else can I do?" She asked tearfully one night.

"We can run away, join another circus, or find work in one of the towns we passed."

"I have no money and no skills. This life is the only thing I have at all. He doesn't pay me to keep the books, he just lets me live, he says, that's payment enough."

"You have me." I said with finality. "You are smart, Donna, you can figure numbers better than the ringmaster himself. You pay the employees don't ya? You keep track of the accounting? Why, I never knew a woman could do such a thing and yet you do."

She reached to hug me, but someone had followed us, and now approached my supply car. It was the original strongman who was demoted to the tents.

"So what do we have here?" he asked with a sneer.

"We're just friends, buzz off," Donna yelled at him.

Why did everything happen when we were setting up for a show, I wondered? Why couldn't we be enroute during such times when there was an opportunity to take a leap of faith by jumping off the boxcar?

We were summoned to the ringmaster, who had a group of important looking men beside him. He told Donna to show one of the men around, but we all understood what this meant. Just as I understood he was trying to provoke me. Because I didn't rile at the thought, he changed his mind and asked, rather, he told Donna she would service this particular man in front of our peering eyes. I went ballistic. I lunged at the man and grabbed him by the throat; three large fellows were upon me in an instant, punching me and pulling me off their cohort. The ringmaster sat back and watched his star attraction be ridiculed and beaten down by his cronies. True to form, it took about seven of them to keep me away from the man who inserted himself into Donna while we all watched.

I was sick, sick with fear and loathing. I hated the ringmaster and felt if given the opportunity I could kill him with my bare hands. I was playing with fire by loving Donna and he wanted to be sure I knew that she belonged to him. I closed my eyes at the sight of the woman I loved being humiliated and prostituted right in front of me.

"Open your eyes, Strongman," the ringmaster said.

I was assaulted with chains, fists, pieces of wood; anything and everything the men could use against me they did. But no matter what torture they imposed, I did not and would not open my eyes.

The following morning, the trapeze troupe found me in a ditch. They needed a large amount of space to train and, when they heard a moaning, they followed it to me. The girl who held the swinging iron ring with nothing but her teeth before being catapulted to the high wire rolled me over. My face was unrecognizable. She called to her mama who came at once and began issuing orders to her group. I was disguised by the drapes and scarves they used in their act and carried back into my original sleeping quarters. There I was nursed back to health, unbeknownst to the ringmaster.

Janey and Sandra, the women who helped nurse me back to health, understood that I needed to speak with Donna. Try as they might, they were never able to catch her alone. The ringmaster had her on guard wherever she went. He presumed I was dead and long gone, and so did Donna. Perhaps it was better to let her think this, but no, I had to find a way to get a message to her.

Janey had me up and about quite a bit now and although the boxcar was confining, I was able to exercise and regain my strength. I was healthy enough that I could jump from the train and make a run for it. I wanted Donna to come with me.

We devised a plan and set it into action. The trapeze team was working on a new show that would include a high wire act. Other circus operations had this but ours was to be more dangerous and alluring.

When the ringmaster was called to witness the daring feat the team wanted to add to their show, he went willingly and took the strongman with him. Donna would be locked in her room until their return. Buster was placed outside Donna's doorway but he was easily lured away with booze and women. We approached the floozies who were all too happy to participate in our plan for the sake of true love.

The plan went off without any problems. The ringmaster was enjoying a daring spectacle while Donna was locked in her room, but the doorman was otherwise occupied, thanks to the floozies. Sparks, a notable felon who joined the circus when running from the law, was great at picking locks, so he came along too. Within twenty seconds, Donna's door was unlocked and our set of "eyes" were on the lookout.

I ran to Donna, who sat on her bed reading a book.

"Jeremy, what in the world, I thought you were dead!" She ran to me and threw herself into my arms.

"We need to leave now. Everyone is occupied; we have ten minutes before we run the risk of being seen."

"Leave? To go where?"

"Anywhere, just grab what you can and let's get out of here." Donna was resistant.

I approached her swiftly, locking my lips upon hers with a passion, but she withheld.

"Don't you want to get out of here? Away from this life, where you are imprisoned?" I asked, motioning to the stifling surroundings in her room.

"More than anything. But he won't allow it, he'll come after me, after us, if he finds out you're alive. If I let you go alone, then you have a real chance, a chance to start over. Otherwise we'll spend our life looking over our shoulders." She began crying, tears marred her makeup revealing pure skin, no bruising this time.

"He'll never change, Donna. He will hit you, beat you within an inch of your life if you take so much as one little misstep. This is your chance at a real life, at love, with me." I was begging.

Donna turned away from me, "It's because I love you that I can't leave. I can endure this, if it means you're safe." She came to me one last time, placing her hands ever so gently on my cheeks, she kissed me softly and I inhaled her scent and memorized this moment. I knew I couldn't change her mind and time was running out.

"If you change your mind, meet me at eleven p.m. at the trapeze car. We can jump together; I will wait until then, but only then, or it will become too risky. Donna, I love you. Please come."

That night I waited for Donna to appear, the clock read ten fifty-five, and the trapeze crew was growing restless beside me. They cared for me but were also anxious to be rid of me so they didn't get in trouble for harboring a fugitive. The ringmaster would have them punished or thrown out in no time.

At ten fifty-six, a flicker of movement caught my eye. "Donna?" I whispered into the dark night.

Donna was pushed in front of me, her mouth taped so she couldn't scream and alert my allies. A gun was to her head, and the ringmaster reeked of booze.

"So it was you she was sneaking about for. Do you take me for an idiot, huh? Do you?" He kept one hand on the gun pointed at Donna and the other he motioned with to showcase the fact he wasn't alone. His henchmen were at his sides and ready to kill me this time for certain. I couldn't waste a single second. If I tried to have Donna released, she would be killed. I jumped from the train and ran for twelve hours straight. I know several men jumped after me, but in the dark of night, it was hard for them to follow me. I could hear their feet hitting the ground as they trailed behind me and hear as their heavy breathing started to slow them down, they were out of shape, and I could outrun them easily. I ran until after the sun came up and landed in the city of Albany.

I slept in a ditch with one eye open during the day and at night walked into a saloon asking for work. I was employed as a doorman and I became a drunk; I loathed every man who walked through the saloon doors; soon enough I was fired for taunting the customers. I took up with the bums, slept on the streets, ate garbage, and drank myself to oblivion. I didn't care what happened to me. Then one day, I woke up and the fella next to me was stiff and grey. His death shocked me into action. I cleaned myself up, got free from booze, and got a job in a barnyard working with animals. The irony was not lost on me; my first exposure to animals was less than pleasant during the circus.

My snakebite scar became a badge of honor, field hands and horsemen alike asked me to see it. Jockeys who rode the horses in the great Saratoga race went out of their way to find me and rub shoulders with me for luck. Any man who could survive a bite from a rattler was lucky. I started believing I was lucky too, my fortune was turning around, and I was earning a fair wage. I would save my earnings and devise a way to get Donna back.

I sat up all night one particular evening figuring out how I could go about this. First, I had to find the circus; they traveled across the country and I would need a few horses and good men to ride out with me and track them down. Sometime during the night, a rattle started in my chest. The hacking didn't keep me fully awake, but the following day I felt like hell. I went to work, but my boss took one look at me and sent me home. Home was a one-bedroom apartment in Saratoga overlooking the racetrack. I stayed in bed for two weeks, my cough progressing to flu-like symptoms, my limbs too heavy to lift. I dropped weight and felt generally weak all over. My boss came to see me.

"You look like hell, Joe." I took on the name Joe when I came to Albany, so no one would be the wiser if anyone came looking for a strongman named Jeremy.

"I feel worse," I told my boss.

"Have you been to the doctor?" he asked, kindly.

"No, sir, I haven't. I am afraid I just don't have the strength."

"I could sure use you at the track. Let me send our doc over here to have a look. Keep your door open, son, we'll get you back on your feet." I was moved to tears by the kindness of this man, a man I barely knew. He followed through and sent a doctor that afternoon. The diagnosis was not at all what I expected.

"Tuberculosis," the doctor stated as a matter of fact. I shut my eyes and muttered the diagnosis to myself. Wondering where in the hell I contracted this disease. Donna was perfectly healthy, as were most of the circus performers. Thinking back, I remember Kitty and Roy, one of the couples in the trapeze act lying about all day, coughing and hacking up blood. Janey cleaned their spittoons regularly, but no one else was sick and I suppose I was naive.

"What's this mean, Doc?" I asked.

"It means if we don't get you to a sanitarium, and soon, you'll wither away."

I was taken to the Saranac Lake Sanitarium the following day. A bed was provided for me by the founder himself, Dr. Trudeau. Imagine my terror when I found out there was a special house for circus folk. I was terrified someone from Barnum would be there and kill me in my sleep. I was a hunted man and didn't have the strength to protect myself any longer. Luckily, the only member from my show was Benny the unicyclist. He was in worse shape than I was, and he only slapped me on my back when I was seated beside him.

"She's all right," he said, and that was the last time we spoke of Donna.

CHAPTER 15

LOVE AND LOSS

Christine reminded me of Donna. She didn't have bruises or an ample bosom, no, but what she had was an attitude, an "it's me against the world" attitude. She possessed a strength and courage I admired greatly. Christine had a laugh that made everyone else feel her joy, her smile was brilliant, and she wore her heart on her sleeve.

"What's wrong, Christine?" I asked one afternoon when we were projecting costs for the upcoming festival.

"My husband won't come. He won't endanger the children and I really hoped to see Joey, he's getting so big, he may even be crawling by now."

"What does Collette say?" I asked.

"She thinks it's for the better. She's afraid if her father comes he will take her away and she wants to stay longer with me."

"She's a good daughter. Besides, I was thinking she had six more months until she was cleared for release."

"She is, but Joe, she is doing so well and I don't want her holed up here just because of me. I want her to go out and see the world."

"She will, when she's ready. Besides, the doctor needs to release her before she can leave."

"I know," she said addressing the realization that her daughter had to stay put a little longer. Before adding, "Do you really think so though, that she'll put herself out into the world, after so much pain?"

"I do, I think she is still mourning over Simon, and probably feels guilty you are positive now. I think she wants to take care of you for the moment and is content in doing so."

"She does. She's even talked about attending the nursing college so she can obtain a degree and return to attend me personally." Christine grew misty. She was overwrought with guilt and pain. I put my hand out and reached hers, not sure how she would react to such an intimate gesture. She grabbed at my hand with both of hers and laid her head on my shoulders. I reached for my hanky and dabbed at her eyes.

"It will be okay, Christine. Maybe she'll meet a doctor who will sweep her off her feet!" That drew a laugh.

"My daughter, married to a doctor. Well, everything for a reason I suppose."

"I suppose," I agreed, searching her eyes to see if we were sharing something beyond mutual friendship. Christine held my gaze, squeezed my hand and then I pulled her toward me. Our lips met and a tingle went down my spine. Her soft upper lip gently grazed mine and she didn't pull away as I suspected she might. Instead she stood, never letting go of my hand and led me to her cottage, Little Red. Once inside she locked the door. We didn't speak, just loved one another, each movement held greater meaning, for the two of us understood loss and love better than most.

COLLETTE

CHAPTER 16

❧

FALLING LEAVES

I held the thermometer beneath my tongue for precisely three minutes, closed my eyes and counted out sixty seconds three times in my head.

"One one thousand, two one thousand, three one thousand..." I was obsessive about my temperature readings more so than the sputum collections, blood pressures, or the weekly weigh in.

"What does it register today, Miss Taft?" I asked my regular nurse as she tilted the instrument at an angle to get the best reading. She could divide the instrument's graduation into tenths and those into tenths easily as a result of so much practice.

"Ninety-eight point seven," she replied, before shaking the mercury in the thermometer back down to its starting point and wiping it clean with alcohol on a cotton ball.

"Excellent," I replied, aware that was a good reading to begin the day with. I was varying now between ninety-eight point five degrees and ninety-nine point one degrees. In addition to my formal chart for the doctor, I was keeping my own charts in my diary. It seemed to me that whenever I was due for my monthlies, my temperature rose, otherwise it stayed in the normal range.

I dared to say I felt almost normal once more. I didn't like to give myself false hope, but for seven months my sputum's bacilli stain has been clear of blood and bacteria indicating my overall health was good. Promise, is a word loaded with implications. I promised Simon before he passed, when we both knew the end was near, that if I continued to progress I would live a full and normal life. I can't, however, bear the thought of leaving my mother alone in the Sans, yet I feel torn because I yearn to see new places and meet new people. All the books I've read while here are about other people and their stories, and finally it could be time to create my own story. I dream of becoming a nurse. I wish to further my education and study anatomy, biology, chemistry, and math. Then, I could come back to the Sans and assist the doctors in procedures such as a forced pneumothorax and thoracoplasties. I could build Spica casts and be far more useful than I am now. As it stands, I help with the children whenever I am able. The Sans children inhabit a cottage dedicated solely to them. The patients vary in age from two through seventeen and have varying degrees of tuberculosis as well as types.

The children tug at my heartstrings in a most peculiar way. They sleep in desolate rooms with whitewashed walls and plain white comforters. While some of the children keep photographs and books on their bedside stands, the environment lacks a cheerfulness I believe they need. I attempt to bring color into their life by affixing watercolors and still-life sketches temporarily to the walls surrounding their beds. In addition to this small improvement, I decided to make it a point to chat with Lena's Thursday night knitting club. If every child could have their own colorful afghan, their bedrooms would be cozier and less institutional.

I often took over for the children's nurse when difficult surgical procedures were being attempted in either the surgical suites or in patients' own homes. I learned to chart, take specimens, as well as vital signs, and enjoyed the work very much.

More than half of the children at the Sans were well enough to attend the Friday night performances all summer long and into the fall; provided it wasn't snowing, we could still be outdoors. As a special treat, the children were given baskets full to the brim of freshly popped corn ladled with butter and salted lightly. To drink, they enjoyed white milk that was sweetened with sugar. These same children were allotted thirty minutes daily to play outside at the playground Dr. Trudeau installed, giving them a sense of normalcy. Not only could they swing and slide, but there was a thicket of blackberry bushes planted beside the playground begging to be thinned during the growing season. Often by the end of their time outdoors, their tiny fingers were stained blue from the berries' sweet juices.

Unfortunately, some children were too ill to leave their beds at all. One sweet girl, Amy Bomke, who was just seven years old, came to the Sans this past year. She tried putting on a brave face, but I could tell she was terrified. She had no family and was all alone at the Sans. I overheard that her entire family perished, thus she was here as a charity case. I often spent my free time reading to her, braiding her soft blond hair, or just sitting by her side playing dolls with her. Her eyes held fear and this showed itself in the violet hollows beneath them. It was lonely and frightening to be in a sanitarium, even one as well intentioned as ours. In the stillness of the night, after the medical staff closed all the doors, fear crept in. Poor, dear child, could she ever recover? I wondered.

Amy had tuberculosis of the spine, which the staff referred to as extra pulmonary, meaning it was not in her lungs but rather had the potential to affect the brain, kidney, bones, joints, or spinal fluid. Amy had a special wheelchair that kept her torso immobile at all times. She wore a partial body cast that extended from the tops of her shoulders to just above her hip. Her bed had a particular orthopedic frame that helped keep her immobile.

"You were far worse when you arrived, Collette." The doctor had come in behind me to check his smallest patients and startled me. He wore his white lab coat over a buttoned-down white shirt with crisp collar and orange bow tie. His high forehead could not hide the fact he was balding. He had spectacles that fell down his nose when he spoke and he was forever readjusting them.

"Pardon me, Dr. Trudeau. I will get out of your way." I stepped lightly aside so that he could examine Amy.

"You're no bother, in fact, I think you're just what the doctor ordered for many of these children."

"How so?" My curiosity was piqued.

"You have wonderful bedside manner. They respond to you," he said, while making notations in his chart.

"Why, thank you, doctor. It's certainly no problem; I find the children to be so endearing."

"Collette, I heard you were thinking of attending a nursing school, is it true?" Doctor Trudeau tucked his pen into his lab coat pocket and held my gaze.

"I would like that, yes, my secondary education was completed before I grew too ill. However, I am aware I can't attend until my symptoms have arrested for a year." I responded honestly to his question.

"Yes, that is true, but in four months, I suspect you will have that clean bill of health and can go out into the world and accomplish your dreams."

"Doctor, do you really suppose so?" I searched his eyes for an honest answer.

"I certainly don't want to get your hopes up, Collette, but I believe you are on the road to recovery. Furthermore, I think you will make a fine nurse. Until then, I'd be honored if you continued to visit the children, you give them hope."

"I would like nothing more," I answered, earmarking the page in *The Adventures of Huck Finn* that Amy and I were reading until her afternoon rest period was over. The hours from two p.m. through four p.m. were deadly still and quiet at the Sans. Everyone was required to rest during this time; no children could be heard, no dogs barked, everyone respected the time frame.

Later that evening, when I was tucked neatly into my own bed, I pulled my diary out from my bedside drawer and grabbed my steel pen, a gift from father last month along with a box of chocolates that I, of course, shared with my friend Evelyn.

> Dearest Diary,
>
> I am to become a nurse! I haven't even told my mother yet. Peculiar, I went to see her at Little Red and the door was locked. I swore I heard a rustle within, no matter, I will tell her the good news tomorrow. If only I had been a nurse for Simon, my beloved. We wished to marry and have our own children one day. He made me promise him that I would move on with my life, he knew he wasn't progressing like the rest of us. He held me to him when we kissed, he was my first love and I shall never forget his sweet embrace. I am not sorry I lost my virginity to Simon, it was my gift to him.
>
> I was worried our tryst would have left me pregnant, but my monthlies have come. For the longest time, I didn't have them when I was ill, but now they are regular, one more sign I am working my way back to good health. I admit I am growing restless without Simon. I miss having someone special in my life, but I am grateful I had him, even if it was for a short while.

A nurse, imagine me in my white cap, it's so thrilling. I can hardly wait to share this news with my mother. Good night, Diary, I will fill my time now with correspondence to father and the boys telling them the good news.

Temperatures today were ninety-eight point nine both morning and evening. I am slightly concerned but Dr. Trudeau says small fluctuations are normal. I weigh in at one hundred and twenty-two pounds and my height remains sixty-eight inches.

Yours truly, Collette

Father was less than pleased upon receiving my letter describing my intentions when cleared. I assumed incorrectly that he would be excited and supportive of my adventure into nursing but instead he feared I would grow ill again. He wanted me as far away from the sick patients as I could get. Father didn't understand what it was to have compassion. I felt a calling toward this work, and although I didn't want to disobey him, Mother said I needed to give his opinion serious consideration. She worried that my father would shun me at home if I went against his wishes. She, however, couldn't hide her excitement at the thought of me in nursing school.

It wasn't just my eventual reinvention that filled my mother with joy, no, she had a glow about her lately that I owed to Big Joe. She took the cure alongside him these days, side by side they read books, played checkers, or cards; their favorite game was bridge. Occasionally, Mother dozed off and I caught Joe staring at her fondly. On more than one occasion, I came upon them holding hands. I began to wonder if something was brewing between the two, and God forgive me because while I understand anything beyond a friendship would be adulterous, I wanted my mother to have someone who cared about her as only a man could. Joe was a good and kind man, and I believe it was love I caught in his eyes.

I left them alone and went about my usual activities, which included cleaning the specimen jars in the laboratory after the doctor had completed his studies, and charting. While rinsing with soap and then patting the containers dry, one of the younger architects who had come to help design the new cottages and structures approached me. He was investigating the layout of the laboratory as he would each and every building and cottage on the property.

"How do you do, miss?" he asked kindly, bowing slightly.

"Why fine, thank you, sir, you are?" I asked, startled by this stranger's appearance.

"I am Will, Will Stafford. I will be here for a year or more to help with the planning and building of the new facilities. I wonder if you'd be willing to show me around a bit." His eyes held a hopeful gaze, but I was taken back by his forwardness. I felt flustered immediately.

"Why, I am terribly sorry, Will, but I can't. The doctor will show you around, I suppose. Good day." I tucked my hair behind my ear and pretended to be very busy as I walked off in the opposite direction. I could feel Will staring after me as I proceeded out the door. I smoothed the wrinkles from the sky blue cotton skirt I chose to wear that day and continued on my way to visit Amy. Afterwards, I went to Mother's and I told her about this interaction. Mother smiled widely, "You are a lovely young woman, Collette, suitors will start calling on you once more, just as Simon did."

"Yes, but, Mother, these men are healthy, I couldn't risk it, I wouldn't risk it." I began sobbing in Mother's lap. I didn't want to grow old alone, a spinster, but I also didn't expect any healthy man to want me.

"It's okay, let it go. I know how deeply you cared for Simon, I do. It'll be all right." She scratched my back and soothed me by rubbing and playing with my hair.

Once I was contained, I shook off my concerns, deciding only to focus on the here and now as she suggested, and was off to take my own rest. My cure chair was comfortable and sat next to Evelyn's. She was absent today, so I took my rest alone, allowing my eyes to close and for my body to be lulled by the hypnotizing sounds of the streams.

Dear Diary,

November has brought with it the snow. Everyone is involved with planning the Thanksgiving pageant that we will celebrate with all the trimmings on November the twenty-fourth. The meal is to be preceded by a short play at noon. Everyone will have had their morning rest and will be fit to take part in their role. I am to play the wife of a settler, learning to prepare a proper feast.

My mother is on the decorating committee and her team has made our surroundings very festive indeed. Cornstalks are tied to each and every banister and entryway; pumpkins and mums are clustered on bales of hay in front of every cottage and building.

Luckily, my temperatures have remained steady; all week I woke with ninety-eight point six degree readings, and went to bed with ninety-eight point eight degree readings. Dr. Trudeau says consistency is what we are after.

Mother was right. I have had more than one gentleman approach me in the last month. First, Will who I fear I was rather rude to, then a young doctor in training named Bernard. Bernard was quite handsome, in a devilish way, but he was less than patient with the children, frightening them with his abruptness and seriousness. I am not ready, Diary. I can't bear to think of anyone but Simon. He was my one and only true love.

I have made my decision, Diary, I don't want to be a teacher or secretary as father insists, I want to be a nurse and so it is settled. I will start my applications this week. I need to include a letter of recommendation, along with letters of merit and documentation of a clean physical exam. Doctor Trudeau said he would oblige me with all of the above.

It's getting late, Diary, tomorrow will be upon me soon enough and I will write once more.

Yours truly, Collette

"Guess what?" I said to Amy when I was visiting the children several weeks later. I wheeled her out through the corridor to the corner of the porch where the sun was shining the most. Heliotherapy was another treatment the doctor ordered and I felt the sunshine treatment did wonders for the spirit.

"What?" she asked me in her gentle, slightly nervous voice.

"I am going to become a nurse! I start my classes in January!" Just saying the words out loud tickled me and I giggled like a schoolgirl.

"But how, I thought you were like me? I thought you had the plague too?" she asked, confused, gripping her dolly tightly.

"I do. I did. My specimens have been clear for ten consecutive months now, which means I am almost considered cured. If you keep taking your rest like a good girl, you may be cured as well."

"Oh. I would love to be a nurse, Miss Collette. Do you think I could be some day?" The child looked up at me with her gray-blue eyes, hope and promise brimming in the form of tears. She took the sleeve of her resting gown and wiped at her eyes.

"I don't see why not. I will make you my own special patient and take extra good care of you until I leave so we can get you better. How are you coming along with your ABCs?" Amy had a tutor who came in and sat with her every day from ten a.m. to noon; because she was not ambulatory she was tutored alone. She couldn't practice her penmanship because any movement was too risky, instead, she was read aloud to and she became both an auditory and visual learner.

"Fine, I am good at addition and subtraction," she stated, rather pleased with herself.

"Excellent. Keep up on your arithmetic as well as your alphabet, so you can be a nurse when you grow up, just like me."

Amy fluttered her eyes with excitement, although she had no casts on her arms, clapping could disturb the spine itself and alter it so she expressed her enthusiasm with her eyes or by wiggling her toes.

"Thank you, Miss Collette. When will you be back?" She asked, with a look of terror creeping across her delicate face.

I held onto her little fingers and gave them a squeeze. "After my lunch, I will stop in to see you before your rest, how would that be?" I asked.

Her eyes held relief; I was becoming this little girl's family and a feeling of overwhelming concern for her coursed through my veins. Noting her brittle nails and thick, lackluster blond hair, I realized in that precise moment that family wasn't always born, sometimes it is was made from shared experiences, like this one. I felt a kinship with Amy; her teeth were chattering so I covered her legs with her comforter and smiled at her before going on my way.

Amy was the only patient at the Sans with spinal TB. The doctor explained her case in depth to me because of the amount of time I spent with her. The most important factor for her treatment lay in her stabilization. If not kept stable at all times, she could suffer from the destruction of bones, or worse, the collapse of her vertebra, which would lead to deformity. It was necessary that she get plenty of rest and decrease the amount of weight bearing down on her diseased vertebrae, hence the need for her cast. It was hard to imagine a child of seven not growing restless in such a scenario, but I heard the doctor talking to her on one such occasion when she was feeling sullen. He said, "Amy, none of us ask for TB, but we do have a choice in how we respond to it. I choose to be happy despite it. How about you?"

From that moment on, Amy was never despondent, but always content and accepting of her fate. She made a choice to be happy despite her condition and that made everyone around her treat her with respect and compassion but never pity. She didn't want or warrant pity.

I often spent my mornings discussing Amy's case with my mother over breakfast. Mother thought Amy was a remarkable child, a true testament to the Sans approach to healing. She remarked time after time, "One must always be optimistic, never doubtful, for without hope where would we all be?"

After breakfast and tending the children, I took my own four-hour period of rest. I closed my eyes during this time and allowed myself to dream of Simon. I recalled his poetry and remembered his touch, our trysts, and the sweet love we shared. It was sacred and transcendent, for I loved him as much now as I did when he was alive. After my rest period, I was free to roam the grounds or spend time with task work; in my case, I sketched and painted landscapes. I always reserved an hour or two after this to be by my mother's bedside in the afternoon. She was assigned eight long hours of rest daily and I knew all too well how lonesome that could get.

"Good afternoon, Mother," I said, as I approached her from behind one cloudy afternoon.

She was holding a crumpled letter in her hands and looked sullen. She passed me the latest letter from my father so that I could see for myself what he had written. The greeting in Father's letters to Mother had changed from "My dearest darling wife, Christine," to "My Dear," and now to simply "Christine." The body of the letter had only one paragraph and in it father spoke mostly of the weather. In his closing, he did mention that Joey and the boys were thriving, but beyond that he only spoke of his latest work project and how busy it was keeping him. He said he'd write more when time permitted, but all his letters had become impersonal drafts.

Mother and Father had spent two painstaking years apart now, but the distance wasn't just physical. I wondered if they had fallen out of love with each other, or in love with others. I would bet money that my father was in love with the woman who cared for his sons, Quinn. My brother alluded to this in a letter to me, he said something along the lines of father spending his free time with the nanny rather than he and his brothers and this made him sour.

"I am sorry, Mother, I know it troubles you not to have more detail regarding the boys." I stood behind her with a brush and gently stroked her hair. It was once a rich brown, but was now a dull, flat brown streaked with gray. She kept it shoulder length and often tucked it behind her ears where it was most comfortable.

"Let's not discuss your father anymore. It is apparent he is moving on with his life, and we shall too." She set the letter into her garbage can and turned toward me. "I'd much rather talk about you. You look so pretty today."

"Thank you for the compliment, Mother. I feel pretty today." I had a rosy hue to my cheeks and was keeping weight on my bones, I even felt slightly curvaceous in my dress, which was a tight fitting number with lavender bodice and deep plum skirt with bustling in the back.

"How are you? Really?" Mother asked placing her hand atop mine.

"I am afraid but hopeful all at the same time. I am excited that I may reinvent myself and become a nurse, but sad to leave you, and this magical place. More than anything, I feel guilty leaving you. If it weren't for me, you wouldn't be here at all." I gazed around my surroundings and I couldn't imagine another place more serene and picturesque or leaving Mother here alone.

"Pish, posh, and nonsense. I am fine here and you'll be so busy you won't have time to miss me!" Mother answered, as her eyes grazed the pendant I wore around my neck. It was a gift from Simon, a simple gold chain with a pea-sized emerald amulet.

Mother did not wish to see me misty, so she subtly changed the subject to the upcoming festival she was co-chairing with Joe. So far, everything was on task.

"People are in a tizzy about the festival. Joe and I may be ambitious in our forecast but, if you can keep a secret, I will tell you what we project."

"I can keep a secret, Mother, please tell me."

"We actually think if everything goes off as planned we can raise several thousand dollars, enough to build half a dozen more cottages like Little Red, or two to three larger nursing cottages. Everyone is chattering on and on about the acts and entertainment, not to mention the wares we will be selling."

"Mother, that's wonderful news!"

"Then why are you frowning?" she asked.

"I wish I could be here for it, but if I am given my clean bill of health…"

"When you are given your clean bill of health," Mother interjected.

"Yes, when I am given my clean bill of health, I won't be here, instead I'll be in a classroom dissecting frogs, or worse, hens!"

"It fills me with such happiness, Collette, thinking of you out in the world, away from this place, as majestic as it is. The fulfillment of your dreams is the eventual fulfillment of mine."

I started growing misty once more, so I rose and took my leave. Mother sat in her cure chair on her porch with her knitting needles at the ready to complete the lap blanket she was making.

"One more thing, Mother. Do you have anyone in mind for the lap blanket?" I asked.

"Why, no I don't, I am just making it to fill my time."

"Do you think I could have it for Amy then? The yellow palette is so bright and chirpy; I think it's just what she needs to make her space homier."

"Absolutely, when you come back tomorrow I will have it done."

"Thank you! If you are able to make more for the other children, they would love it. I am speaking to Lena this afternoon about this as well."

> Diary,
>
> I am even more perplexed at present. Mother seems to be getting herself entwined with a man at the Sans. He is a very kind man, but I don't know whether or not to admit to her what I have seen. Help me, Diary,

for while I am glad for Mother, I am unaware how to handle such a situation.

I went to bring her a dessert unexpectedly this evening and heard the muttered sounds of two lovers entwined.

Diary, I have only one month left until I will be cleared. My temperatures, sputum collections, bowels, and blood pressures continue to be normal and what's more is that I feel alive. I want to be up and about and grace each morning with purpose.

I shall spend the Christmas holiday here at the Sans and then prepare for my departure.

I have come to love little Amy. She is like a sister to me; she is up and down with her vitals as is my mother. I wish they would be paired together, for I do believe Mother would take her under her wing. She is a bit like Emma Darling the way her mind wanders into daydreams.

I will think on this today, Diary.

Yours, Collette

I have a month until I am cleared. When I walk across the campus housing the buildings everyone claps and cheers for me, giving me the encouragement I need to move forward from the place that has become my home for over a year. My clearance slip will be the best present I could dream.

I spoke with Mother about her budding romance and she admitted that she did indeed love Joe. Father wrote a private letter to her detailing his relationship with the nanny and how they wish to marry which means my parents will be getting a very unprecedented divorce. Father spoke to the priest and a judge regarding this matter and due to the precarious circumstances, they would be granted an annulment.

Mother didn't feel the need to rush into a wedding ceremony with Joe but they had moved in together at Little Red as I suspected. The doctor, myself, and a few other staff members were the only ones who knew about this arrangement. No one wanted to accuse them of living in sin, and who could blame them for finding love and happiness in such dire circumstances?

The days leading up to my final testing passed by quickly. The upcoming holidays had everyone in cheerful moods; the cooks baked chocolate pinwheel cookies and snickerdoodles and gave them to us as gifts in tins wrapped with ribbon. Each cottage had its own pine tree whose scent wafted throughout our spacious confinement. Ours was a Douglas fir, the girls in my cottage, who had swiftly become my dearest friends, decorated the tree with ornaments we made during our task time. Some of us painted the tips of pine cones in bright hues, others made cushioned ornaments that looked like pies, and some gathered twigs and sticks to make sleighs, and so on.

We drew names for each other and on Christmas Eve, we each received one gift from someone in our cottage. I received a beautiful pair of gray cashmere gloves, knit for me by Evelyn.

Father sent Mother and me gift-wrapped parcels. We opened new shawls, bolts of fabric, books, and stationery boxes. I felt guilty because so many of my roommates weren't as fortunate as I was, so I shared my gifts with everyone and the holidays were merry for all.

One week left and my tests remained clear. I spent long expanses of time reflecting on my first moments at the Sans, the lengthy and monotonous days were so boring and quiet initially. I kept records of squirrels, sketched the flora and fauna around me, and even counted the leaves on trees to pass the time. I was always exhausted and sleep came naturally. I slept so much of my youth away, in fact, that I wished to limit myself to seven hours per day henceforth. My tiny room would go to another, so I decided now was as a good a time as any to begin packing my meager belongings.

The books I amassed would go to the circulating library, all but the red leather bound diary that was once Emma Darling's, and *Little Women*, given to me by our friend in Skaneateles, Mrs. Putnam. Otherwise, *The Tanglewood Tales*, *Jack and Jill*, *Huck Finn* and *Tom Sawyer*, *The Sky Blue*, *Black Beauty* and more would all be donated. I stacked my notebooks by order of date and placed them in the bottom of my suitcase, I wrapped my pens and watercolors in muslin, then placed them beside the sketchbooks. My photographs went in next, followed by my winter skirts, of which I had three. I folded them neatly and lay my shawls atop them, my long sleeve blouses went on the pile next. I left room for my undergarments and the two modest dresses I would rotate this week, along with my personal effects like my brush and mirror. It took me all of an hour to sort my belongings and set them beside my door.

I glanced around my room, my home; it was where Simon and I went against the rules to be alone together and where my body was cured.

Dear Diary,

It is a somber day. I have received devastating news. I am crying as I write, partly because I am sad, but mostly because I am enraged that I allowed myself hope. I could spit nails I am so mad. I hoped with all my being and prayed with all my might that I would be cleared in a few short days. However, my bacilli stains this morning showed disease. My temperatures remain consistent, as does my weight, height, and bowel output measurements. I feel better than I can ever remember. Even as child, I remember the heavy way in which I breathed, simply traversing the stairs to go up to the bedroom I shared with Emma Darling left me out of breath. Here I can walk and stroll and forget I ever had difficulty with my lungs at all. The Magic Mountain, as some of us call it, eases our breathing and instills us with hope.

No one knows this yet. Dr. Trudeau only just left my room. His wife was bringing me a morning meal to my room as they assumed I would wish to process this information alone for the time being.

I thought of my white nurse's cap, and all the courses I dreamed of taking, but then thought of things differently. God must want me to stay, there is a reason I am testing positive after nearly twelve months of negative scans. It must be a sign that I am not to leave, I will stay and that is that.

I will unpack later today, Diary, and won't allow even one moment of self-pity. Amy needs me and so does Mother. Thank you, Diary, for always being here for me. It is a new year.

Yours, Collette

I ate my morning meal of steak and two eggs, washed up, and placed my hair in a nice tight bun at the nape of my neck. I splashed more cool water on my cheeks and eyes, which were swollen from crying. I dabbed them dry with my white cotton towel. I was afraid of walking out my door and into the quad between the cottages for people always cheered me onward and wished me well in my future as I passed them by. I didn't want to disappoint anyone or take away their hope, but the reality was, I was staying. Best to get it over with I suppose.

"Mother?" I called out as I knocked gently on her door. Big Joe answered with a grim look and opened the doorway allowing me entry.

Mother was lying on her left side and according to Joe, had been up most of the night coughing and I could tell just by looking at her that she was feverish.

"Joe, may I speak with you outside?" I spoke quietly so as not to disturb my mother.

Once outside, Joe told me that mother was scheduled for surgery after I left. She was doing her best to be brave, but she was in need of a pneumothorax procedure. She didn't want me to know because she knew I wouldn't leave her.

I explained to Joe that I tested positive that morning and the big man pulled me to his chest like the surrogate father he had become.

"Darling girl, I am so sorry to hear that. You must be beside yourself." Joe held me in his strong embrace for a moment longer.

"Actually, Joe, I am okay. I worked it out in my mind that God had a different plan for me. He wanted me here for some reason so here I will stay. I will go in and tell Mother now, unless you think I should wait?" I asked.

"I suppose there is no time like the present." Joe waited on the porch, while I went to my mother to tell her the jarring news.

"Mother, how are you feeling?" I sat beside her on her cot.

She turned toward me and tried with all her might to look well and behave as such, but even the tiniest movements spurred coughing fits. I cupped my hands and patted her back to bring forth the sputum that was clogging her airways. When the fit was over, Mother was exhausted. I didn't have the heart to tell her my news, but I had to.

"Mother, I have news to share. Can you sit up for a moment?" I asked, ready to plump her pillows and raise her to a sitting position.

Her face was drained of color, highlighting her age, her hair was in a rat's nest about her head, and the hollows beneath her eyes were dark and swollen. My inner dialog and heart didn't want to stress Mother any further with my sorrowful news, yet my mind knew I had to tell her.

"Collette, it's so lovely to see you today, are you all packed?" she asked.

"Actually, Mother, that's what I wanted to talk to you about." A look of concern came across her face and she fiddled with her fingers.

"I spoke with Dr. Trudeau earlier today and, well, my sputums weren't clear this morning. He can't give me a clean bill of health unless they are clear for a year. He is advising that I stay on for another year and keep up with my normal routines and activities. Stress could have induced it, or perhaps, as I told Joe, I am meant to stay by your side. I am meant to stay here, at the Sans, with the people I love."

"Then why?" She began asking the question I asked myself over and over again. Why was I inactive for nearly a year?

"Dr. Trudeau believes my positive emotions have a naturally occurring effect on my health. He thinks my optimism and hope have kept me clear, but once I began stressing over nursing school, I became active once more."

Mother's eyes welled over with tears. She had no words, and couldn't adequately express her grief. I told her I was okay with the news, that I was in no rush to leave her side, or the beautiful surroundings that have become my home. Then I changed the topic to her upcoming surgical procedure. It was scheduled for the following week and I would be right by her side the entire time.

Mother squeezed my hands tight, and I fixed her blankets.

"Would you like to move to the porch, Mother? It's lovely outside, the sun is shining but it's not too warm."

"No, dear, I think I'll sleep some more. But thank you. Joe will stay with me if I decide to go out later."

"Okay, I need to go see Amy, but will be by later." I kissed my mother's hands and squeezed them tight before leaving.

I left Little Red with a sense of dread at seeing my mother so undone and sickly. I needed to speak with Dr. Trudeau about the procedure and its outcomes, but first, I had to get word to Father not to send a carriage for me.

CHAPTER 17

❧

A NEW HOME

The pneumothorax procedure was simple in theory, but not in execution. It involved the surgical collapse of the lung, which doctors believed allowed the lung's cells time to heal. Any holes in the lungs caused by the tuberculosis would spontaneously close and then heal, allowing for healthier chest cavities.

Air was forced through a long needle between the ribs into the patient's pleural cavity surrounding the affected lung. The lung was then collapsed, much like a balloon, and allowed to sit and rest upon itself in the chest. As the body absorbed air, it refilled itself, causing the need for numerous repeats of the procedure throughout a six to eight month period. Some patients required years of the treatment, or opted eventually for a permanent lung collapse, but Mother's diagnostic treatment period was shorter and she wouldn't require such measures.

Miss Taft, Dr. Trudeau's assistant, assured me he was an expert at this procedure and that he was not only gentle but also precise. However, there were serious side effects. The first thing we needed to watch for was bleeding; if a vessel were cut during the insertion of the needle, bleeding could result.

Most often the bleeding stopped spontaneously, but if it didn't the doctor needed to treat it as an emergent case. Secondly, we needed to observe my mother for signs of subcutaneous edema; if her neck, face, or chest began to swell it could mean the pleural air was leaking into the tissue, which again would require a call to the doctor. Otherwise, Mother would simply rest and allow her tissues to heal.

I wrote a letter to my father while we prepped my mother emotionally for her upcoming surgery. I asked, no begged, for his help. I thought if Mother had a place of her own to heal, where I could be with her at all times, things would be easier. I had never asked my father for anything until now and what I asked was no small favor. I wanted a house. I wished for a home where my mother, Joe, Amy, and I could live together as our own hodgepodge family. I truly believed in my heart that together we would thrive better than we did separately. The sanitarium cottages were an excellent facility for those without means for their own place in town. But we had the means, or, rather, Father did. He was a filthy rich man, and I felt certain he would oblige his only living daughter in this request.

Father surprised me with his immediate reply. He was more than willing to build a home in Saranac Lake for us, and planned to visit the town personally to see what properties were available. I told Father I knew of a young, enterprising architect who might be willing to oversee the project. I had seen Will on more than one occasion and we were becoming fast friends.

Will had a sense of what was necessary for a consumptive patient's home; first and foremost was the wraparound porch. Every home in the village had a full porch so the inhabitants could take their cure outside all day, but in their own home. Many town folk hired nurses and cooks to take care of them so they were able to lounge in their cure chairs all day long. Thus, an additional room was often required downstairs beside the kitchen. Homes were designed to allow in as much light as possible, as heliotherapy was highly touted as a cure alongside rest.

Will had begun the property search for me, as my father suggested, and narrowed it down to three locations. One location was smack dab in the center of town where we could easily walk to dine and shop if we were able and willing. The second location was quite remote, albeit, the property was phenomenal. It had an expansive valley that would surround the abode, and it teamed with life. Wild ferns grew all about the property, and the ground was lush with red dirt that was ideal for gardening.

The third property was not as remote and less centralized, but it suited our needs and purposes quite well. The property sat on an acre, and it had a stream running along the edge, bringing the deer and other wildlife within view. It was on top of a small mountain, about a mile from the San's property line. The views were spectacular, the neighbors not too far, and we all agreed it was the place for us.

Father came to town in his carriage, bringing his own partner with him to map out the homestead and consider further developing the area. Saranac Lake was booming as more and more consumptive patients came to live out their lives in the mountain air. More folks were choosing to build their own homes instead of residing at the Sans, which necessitated more doctors and nurses. The fascinating thing about Saranac Lake, the thing that took all of us by surprise, was that folks with tuberculosis were never shunned here. We were allowed to dine alongside healthy folks, shop in the stores without any sideways glances. We could stroll through the village streets and attend church sitting side by side our healthy neighbors.

The town had expanded from just over five hundred residents when we first arrived in 1887 to over fifteen hundred now. Restaurants were constructed, and a real village, similar to Pittsford, New York, where I grew up, was taking shape. Father saw dollar signs and potential, but I also think on some level he felt the call to action.

Meeting with him at our property was bittersweet. Joe and I covered Mother's eyes and told her we had a surprise. We wheeled her, because she was not currently ambulatory, to a carriage that waited to take us to our destination. Once we arrived, we delivered her in the center of what was to become her new home.

We withdrew the handkerchief that was tied around her eyes, and she was startled and overwhelmed to see my father, Will, Joe, and I all standing around staring at her.

"What's this?" she asked, very confused.

"This is your new home, Christine." My father answered, taking steps toward her.

"I am afraid I don't understand," she said, bewildered, wiping at her dripping nose with a handkerchief.

"Mother, Father has agreed to build you, us, our own home, right here. You, Joe, Amy, and I will all live here, together as a family. We will have our very own nurse and cook too."

"My goodness." Mother was overwhelmed by my father's generosity and startled to see him in person after such a long period of time. I sensed the two of them wished to be alone for a moment and gestured for Joe, Will, and father's partner to walk with me.

The gentlemen and I discussed what we would like to see in our home. Will admitted Father wanted us to have all the modern appliances and amenities and we certainly weren't opposed to anything that could make our lives easier to manage.

I glanced at my parents; my father kept several yards of space between himself and my mother as they spoke. He was afraid of tuberculosis for he had seen how it ravaged those he loved. I could tell Mother was whimpering by the way her shoulders rose and fell, and then Father was on the ground in front of her, his head in his hands, crying at long last over all he had lost. TB tore families apart at the very core, and in this precise moment, they were feeling its wrath.

I know my parents loved each other, and always would. I also understood it was time to let go. I don't know exactly what transpired between my folks that afternoon but when we returned to them they both had red-rimmed eyes. Smiling through their pain, they said their goodbyes. My mother held out her hand to Joe, and he came immediately to her side to collect her.

Father and his partner concluded the day with drawings and plans. Will promised to go over them with me the following afternoon at the construction site.

"I will ring you, Collette, and we can discuss any changes or additions you and your mother wish to make. Just keep me informed. Otherwise I'll be back in two months to check on the project." Just like that, Father went home, leaving Will in charge.

Although a new telephone service had been set up at the sanitarium, I still hadn't used it myself. I still couldn't get over this incredible invention. To speak to someone so far away through a system of wires befuddled me. Will and Father were able to communicate about the house this way and I could see in patients' eyes how special it was to hear their loved ones' voices on the other end of the line when they, too, were able to phone a family member. Sometimes that was a better cure than anything.

❀

The fall season brought forth the most vibrant array of colors, it was a sight nothing short of majestic, and to Will, it was life changing. We walked across the property on the aptly named River Street that was soon to be my home, marking off rooms with stakes.

"Perhaps I should build a house of my own here. There is no other place quite like it that I am aware of," Will commented, after partitioning off the kitchen area.

He looked at me, his gaze lingering a bit longer than was comfortable, and declared, "There is no perhaps about it, I have made up my mind. I'd like to spend my life living here. The mountains and streams are perfect for a huntsman like me, and the work is only just beginning. As more and more people come, I will have no trouble bidding for jobs."

Will was talking into the air and to himself more than he was to me. He was like a child in a candy store, giddy with excitement. He was quite charming, truthfully. He had curly golden locks, blue eyes, and a wide grin that was offset by a pair of dimples. He was an inch or so shorter than me, but when he wore his cap we were equally matched.

We continued to map out the house, enlarging the south side one-story porch even more than we originally planned. This porch was slated to have sliding windows, while the upper level porch on the eastern portion of the first floor porch would be left wide open. We stood back together assessing our rough design. The kitchen was in the front of the house so that as you entered from the enlarged porch into a large hallway, it would be immediately on the left. It would be fit with ample workspace and six windows. Three windows looked out onto the front porch and three faced the side porch. A large sitting room was on the right side of the hallway; it would be bright and sunny like the kitchen. Off the back of the house would be a living room, as well as a room for hired help. There would also be a study that we could use to store our books. The bedrooms would be upstairs, four in all. One for my Mother and Joe, one for Amy and me to share, and two extras for visitors.

"What color do you imagine your house will be someday, Collette?" Will asked.

"A sunny color, like buttercups or honey. I'd like pretty green shutters and maybe stone or brick columns. My dream home would have a welcoming red-brick pathway, a white picket fence, and rose bushes everywhere you looked. But this isn't my home; this one will belong to my mother, so we should ask her." I continued to let my mind wander as Will gathered the tools he used for measuring and marking areas.

"Okay, I will do that. I have to order the siding within the next few weeks, but otherwise it looks good. I suppose we better head back." We sat side by side in the carriage on the way back to the Sans, I felt an electrical current where Will's leg briefly touched my dress. I wondered if he felt it too. But when he delivered me to the door, he merely tipped his hat to me and said, "so long." I was wishing for a kiss on the cheek I suppose and when it didn't occur, I felt disappointed.

"Why hasn't he asked me out for a date yet, Mother, Joe?" I asked the sweet couple seated on the porch that evening.

"I'm sure he's afraid you'll turn him down again," Joe said with his gruff laugh.

"Hmmm. It's true, I was rather rude to him when we first met and he asked to be shown around town," I said, scuffing my shoes on the ground.

"Maybe you can offer to show him around now?" Mother suggested.

"I think by now he is familiar with Saranac Lake, Mother, don't you?"

"I think he probably is, but he doesn't know you know that. I'd offer. What harm can come from it?"

"Well, he can turn me down I suppose, and it would serve me right." I paced back and forth wondering what to do.

"Why don't you sleep on it, Collette, you know the doctor said not to overtax yourself."

Mother was right as usual. I had to force myself to get four hours of daily rest on the porch and spent the rest of my days in motion. My mind buzzed like a honeybee, so many things were happening it was hard to sit still. The air had a current of its own because there were so many newcomers to the Sans. We had taken in dozens of individuals from Plattsburgh now that the Chateauguay railroad ran directly to Saranac Lake from this particular town. It had been hit particularly hard by the plague. I helped admit and situate the new patients into their appropriate quarters and said a silent prayer that the funds from the festival could help build these people a cottage of their own.

They weren't all family members, but they shared a common bond that few could understand.

We also had construction crew workers milling about the acreage, figuring out where the best locations would be for irrigation ditches and sanitation stations. The Independent Medical Research Center was nearing its completion and Dr. Trudeau was thrilled. To study bacilli and other bacteria alongside other scientists to further understand the human immune system remained his true lifelong goal.

Additionally, a post office had been constructed in the center of town allowing for a daily mail delivery that came promptly at ten in the morning. Patients received letters from home and went straight to their stationery boxes to begin correspondence of their own.

After the afternoon rest period at the Sans, hammers once more were heard pounding nails into beams, and the scratching sound of saws echoed through the valley. Children laughed and played side by side on the playground, while teens harvested the fruits from the gardens that were extra bountiful this year. Our cook was brilliant at disguising the taste of kale and broccoli in such a way that even the smallest patients ate their fill.

Mother had been clear of her fever for four days, and after a week with normal temperatures, the doctor would perform his third pneumothorax. He spoke confidentially to me that he could permanently collapse the lung that was troubling Mother by crushing the phrenic nerve, thereby paralyzing the diaphragm on one side. But he was willing to try this procedure one more time, because it was less invasive. When the morning of her procedure arrived, I was surprised to find Will milling around outside my cottage. He was waiting to walk with me to Little Red.

"Can I get you anything, Collette?" he asked with a look of concern.

"No, thank you, Will. It's just so kind of you to be here, thank you." We walked together down the pathway that wound itself through the grounds until reaching Little Red. About halfway through our walk, Will sidled up beside me and draped his arm across my back; it was a sweet gesture that I was familiar with. So he had felt the current between us.

"Mother?" I spoke her name into the doorway that was ajar. Joe was kneeling beside her and she was rolled onto her left side. Dr. Trudeau arrived right behind us with his black leather satchel, a series of pumps, and his most trusted nurse, Miss Taft. She assured me that this procedure would go as well as the two previous ones, Dr. Trudeau was, gentle, she said, and her confidence in him settled my nerves.

"Let me get you some tea, Collette." Will suggested. He seemed more nervous that I was.

"That would be kind, Will. I'll take two sugars and one cream, please." I watched him walk toward the central kitchen and wondered about our future. I was not cleared, but oh, how I wished to kiss his lips. I threw the thought aside as quickly as it came because Mother was a bundle of nerves even though she had been through this before. I offered to relieve Joe of his duties by her side, but he wanted to remain with her, so I sat instead rocking back and forth, squeaking against the wide plank wooden porch floors. I closed my eyes as the breeze tickled my nose and forced me to sneeze.

"Achoo!" I sneezed, one, two, three times.

"God bless you! I heard you a mile away." Will presented me with a cup of steaming tea. He took one look inside the room housing my mother and her team of medical staff and fainted right at my feet.

"Will!" I shouted. I splashed him with droplets of tea and luckily, he came to.

"What happened?" he asked, staring up at me from the ground below.

"You fainted!"

"I did?"

"Yes, you did. Here, just sit up slowly. Keep your head between your knees. Are you seeing stars?" I asked.

"No, well, maybe a few," he answered honestly.

"Keep your head down. What happened?" I asked, trying to get his mind off whatever caused him to faint.

"I saw the needle, and it was long. That's all I remember."

I sat beside him, my hand on his shoulder, rubbing his back in circles. I wanted to rub my fingers through his curls and it was all I could do to resist. Something was building with this gentle, kind man, but I didn't want to lead him on. We could never be. He would never want to be with me; I am tainted and he is not. It would be too risky a match. If I cared about him at all, I needed to remove myself.

"Feeling better?" I asked.

"Not yet, I think you better keep rubbing my back, and while you're at it, can you rub my hair too?" he teased as if reading my mind.

"Let's get you up on your feet. Just don't look in there, look at me." I told him.

"That's easy to do, you're beautiful, Collette. Do you know how fond I am of you?" he asked.

I didn't quite know how to respond. This was a peculiar time to be discussing our personal business. But I admit it did take my mind off my mother and her procedure momentarily. I could feel the blush rush to my cheeks and stifled a giggle.

"Are you sure you didn't hit your head on a rock when you fainted?" I asked. We were holding hands now.

"I am sure. Would you reconsider my earlier offer, and perhaps show me around town, maybe dine with me as well?" I saw my reflection in his eyes.

"I would like to Will. But I am afraid I can't."

"Oh." Will replied, stunned.

"I am sorry." I didn't offer any further explanation. My heart was heavy with need and wanting but if I truly cared for him, I had to let him go.

"Well, give my best regards to your mother then, I will be on my way." He looked at the ground, cleared his throat, and left. He walked down the gravel path, away from Little Red and I could feel my heart break. Was Will my second chance at love? It was no matter, for it wouldn't happen, I wouldn't do that to him. I didn't want to saddle anyone with my health issues because it simply wasn't fair. I allowed myself a cry, and Miss Taft came out to see what I was fussing over.

"Your mother will be just fine, dear. Have no worries."

"Yes, I know she will, Miss Taft, thank you for your reassurance."

Of course, she mistook my tears for concern over my mother, as they should have been. I shouldn't be worrying myself over a silly boy at a time like this.

PART TWO

AMY
1900

CHAPTER 18

❦

AMY ON HER OWN

"Wake up, sleepy head!" Nana was standing in my doorway, dressed immaculately in her favorite hunter green full-length skirt, which she paired with a crisp white blouse and bolero jacket. She wore a cameo pinned to her lapel and had tiny pearl studs in her ears. The pearls were a gift from Joe on their wedding night. Her hair was entirely gray now, and she wore it in a bun at all times. Less fuss, she claimed, when it was off her face.

"Five more minutes," I mumbled, trying to block out the sun's bright rays, which shined brightly through my bedroom windows now that Nana had opened my drapes. Nana came further into my room and uncovered me. She made room for herself on my bed and pushed the hair from my eyes, settling a kiss on my forehead.

"Today is your big day. Time to rise and shine." She smiled, her eyes glinted with tears as she stood to leave, but not before folding my afghan, which I still used to cuddle, and placing it at the foot of my bed.

I had butterflies in my stomach already and I hadn't even put my feet to the floor yet. I was nervous about my future but happy to be fulfilling my lifelong dream, finally.

⚜

Thirteen years ago I was brought to the Sans and during all this time, I have never once left Saranac Lake. I spent my first several years in the children's cottage wearing a partial body cast that was itchy and constricting. I remember the itching got so fierce at times, I had to dig my fingernails into my palms as hard as I could to create a sensation elsewhere, drawing my brain away from the real site of nuisance.

I practiced deep breathing, as taught to me by my nurse, Miss Taft, God rest her soul. The breathing did help me to refocus my mind and keep still. That was my first requirement during my growing years. I needed to remain still and immobile so I wouldn't disturb or irritate my spine and run the risk of becoming deformed.

"Stay still, Amy," Miss Taft used to remind me, "or you'll look like the hunchback of Notre Dame." I had spinal tuberculosis, a far less common form of the deadly disease that was the cause of death for my entire family.

I vaguely remember our house in New York City. We lived in the infamous Theater District because my mother was an actress and singer. My father was her manager, booking her on all the best shows. My parents always told me it was love at first sight for them. Once they met, they courted for two weeks and decided not to wait, but to get married right away at the courthouse. Nine months later, my sister Dahlia was born.

Atypical for the times, my mother left the baby with Father during the daytime while she went to rehearse lines and learn the music for her evening performances. She had dozens of roles, but favored any that allowed her to hone her vocal skills. She was a soprano, and a mezzo soprano at that. She could hit the highest high notes and belt the lowest lows, making her a fabulous candidate for the operas and other musical performances that were so popular.

It didn't matter that Mother was pregnant during most of her career, for often she sang behind the curtain. When she did take the stage, it was in an immaculate dressing gown and full make up and regalia that disguised her protruding belly.

My sister Daisy was born next. As always, my father booked and managed Mother's blossoming career while he stayed home to rear his two daughters. He enjoyed this and was more nurturing than my mother. He preferred to be home cooking, cleaning, and taking the children to Central Park in the afternoons, as well as accompanying them to and from school.

Next came Tommy, followed by Benjamin. I was the last child born and they named me Amy Rose.

Our household was boisterous and fun. Mother always hummed and sang as she pranced about the rooms, practicing her lines, donning her newest clothes and jewelry. Our humble beginnings quickly changed for us and Mother grew to develop a following that made her quite a popular star. We moved to Broadway Street and bought an apartment in a high-rise building across from the stage where she most often worked. Now she could simply stroll across the street for her performances and come back home afterward to celebrate her success with us.

When she started feeling nauseous once more, she was less than delighted at the thought of another child and enduring a sixth pregnancy. When she found out that she wasn't pregnant, it was perplexing. The doctor took note of her symptoms; she had seasickness that made her nauseous and motion sickness that made her spin upon standing. She felt a pain deep in her bones and had muscle spasms that most often occurred around her eyes. Later her gait faltered and she started falling more often than not. Her employers ignored the symptoms at first and allowed her to sing from a seated position on stage. But as time went on her pain was too severe to ignore, and her once brilliant sound became stifled and breathy. Paying customers began to complain, so Mother was ordered off the set for a period of three months.

She was prescribed bed rest at once to regain her strength and calm her nerves. Her employers hated to lose a talent like her, so they offered to hold her position while she was nursed back to health.

At the same time, father began coughing in spastic fits, often spitting up blood on his hankies, frightening all of us children. This went on for some time before he took to bed alongside my mother.

The oldest among us, Dahlia, was now seventeen and capable of taking care of the household. Father had taught her well, so when he took to bed beside Mother, no one worried too much.

Dahlia and Daisy handled all the daily household chores, and the boys who were still in school were required to take me daily to and from my classes.

When Dahlia fell ill, Daisy took over. Her first order of business was to summon the doctor once more.

The doctor remained perplexed by Mother's symptoms, but declared father as positive for consumption without any hesitation. My father adamantly denied this was possible; he rarely left home, spent his time indoors, and what's more, was not poor, unclean, or unkempt. Consumption was for the riffraff of the city. It was the bums and city dwellers who slept in slums, shared bottles of whiskey, took up with heathens, and had little regard for personal hygiene who fell prey to consumption.

The doctor corrected father's romantic notions of the disease and diagnosed Dahlia the same way. He left my sister with his list of instructions and gave Daisy a list of symptoms to look for in the rest of us.

One by one we fell. Daisy and the boys both started coughing within weeks of each other. The whole family, everyone but me, was ill and suffering in bed with fevers and tremors. I did my best to listen to instructions and bring water and hardboiled eggs to my ill family members. I ran the dust rag across the counters and tabletops, laundered the clothing, and even swept. It was all getting to be too much, but I pushed on.

That's when Mother passed away quietly in the night. Father was the next to go. He died, we think, of a broken heart more than anything else. My sisters also went quickly, and for that, I was grateful, for my brothers suffered the most. They had raging fevers, gruesome looking spit, coughed all hours of the day and often choked and gurgled up clots of blood thick with mucus-tinged slime.

The doctor declared that everyone in my household was infected in some facet with consumption and that I was the only one spared. A kindly neighbor, who often looked in on me during this time, took me in as her own. I was only six years old at the time of my family's demise. I will always associate the smell of lilacs with that kindly lady, Ms. Swift. Goodness sakes, I don't know if I am making it up, but when I was little I always thought she looked like a peacock. Her hair was so gray it looked blue; she wore loads of purple eye makeup and plum lipstick. Her clothing was feathery and flowing, to hide her ample figure I suppose. Regardless, she took me in and that's what mattered most. It was a desperate time for me and I grew forlorn and introverted.

In my seventh year, I lost my appetite. I had no interest in food, not even pies, pastries, or my favorite sugar cookies. I lost weight and developed back pain so severe that walking became difficult.

Ms. Swift summoned the doctor who diagnosed me after conferring with several specialists. I had skeletal TB. As lovely as this lady was, she didn't want to care for me any longer, so she sent me to the Sans. I wrote to Ms. Swift for many years. She was the only person I had to correspond with since my entire family was dead and I was alone but for her. When she passed on, I was truly alone.

CHAPTER 19

✿

SWINGING HIGH

Alone and afraid, I was transported to the Sans and evaluated by Dr. Trudeau. He concurred that I did indeed suffer from spinal TB, which accounted for fifty percent of the extra pulmonary cases. The most important factor in my case was stabilization.

I was given my own room, complete with a bed, chest of drawers, side table, kerosene lamp, and bookshelf. *Black Beauty* sat waiting for me to flip through and admire when I arrived. However, the first order of business, in my case, was an immobilizing bandage, or cast. I was entombed from shoulders to hip and was forced to remain erect at all times. Reclining, sitting up, or moving around were difficult tasks that required help because I could not bear my body's weight or change positions without assistance.

A nurse or volunteer would support my head with strong hands as I rose each morning and was laid back each night. Even the slightest motion could disturb my vertebrae and cause them to collapse. I was so frightened by this that I accepted the "tomb" and wore it without complaint. Dr. Trudeau taught me early on that I must accept my fate, and that I had a choice, as all humans do. I could be sullen and brood all day because of my condition, which he thought would only make it worse, OR I could accept my TB as part of who I was and be happy that I was alive. He helped me to find beauty in the mundane and as a result, I became quite spiritual from a young age. I still mourned for my family but had hope and faith that I would survive.

I spent eight hours on my back daily as a requirement for my condition because I needed to decrease any weight on my spinal cord. I stared at the ceilings and took to counting things during this time, everything from the number of nails in each board, to the wood grains on the pillars that held up the structure. I prayed fervently during the day and dared to dream of a future. I had a man in my future, he was my knight in shining armor who came to rescue me from my doldrums. I imagined kissing this man and even named our children, two boys and two girls.

The other children in the Sans ignored me. They were allowed to interact with one another on the playground and at social functions, but I was kept in bed, rarely allowed to attend. Any sudden movements could cause havoc, so it was best I remained alone in my quiet space.

Collette came into my life during this time and took me under her wing like she was my very own big sister. One grand afternoon that I shall never forget, Collette told me she had a surprise. She raised me up from a horizontal position, her hand providing the necessary support under my head so that I was now sitting. Next to her was the wheelchair that we used occasionally so that she could tour me around the grounds and help lessen my boredom. This particular day she helped me to my chair and situated me at once, then tied a ribbon around my eyes so I couldn't see where we were going. She led me down a corridor and because my eyes were shielded, my other senses stood at attention, I could smell the apples being churned to sauce as we passed the kitchen. Next, I determined we were headed toward the play yard all the while wheeling through the musty leaves of fall. Once we stopped, Collette undid the ribbon from my eyes and in front of me was a chair hanging from a tree by sturdy ropes. It was more than a swing, because it had an entire backing to it. The doctor and his wife were waiting for me. They settled me into the swing and strapped me in.

"Close your eyes, Amy," The doctor instructed. His wife stood beside him as always.

He drew the chair back and released me. I was swinging! It was miraculous. I could feel the wind sweep through my hair. To feel motion after years of remaining still was beautiful and cathartic. They pushed me higher and because my head was braced there were no concerns. I extended my arms as if I were in flight and for a moment felt a sense of freedom born to few. I laughed until I cried for the sensation was indescribable. My laughter garnered the attention of other children at the playground, several of whom came to see what was causing a scene.

Choruses of "I want to try!" came from the other children. But this was my chair, my swing, my release.

Every day, Collette took me to the swing and pushed me as high as she could. The flutter in my stomach gave way to laughter and fun, and friendships.

Several small girls my age asked to push me and make me laugh. Collette allowed it and over time, we got to know one another. Sally Anne became a friend; after she pushed me she would disappear for a little while and come back with buckets filled with the sweetest blackberries from the thicket behind the grounds. We ate and laughed together until my allotted time of thirty minutes was over and I had to go back to a horizontal position to ease my vertebrae.

The swing was among my greatest gifts. The feeling it evoked and the hope it garnered for a young girl meant more to me than anything else in the world.

Collette and I grew very close when she took me on as her patient. Although she wasn't a nurse as she had hoped to be, she was my nurse and did the very same things the women in white caps did. She visited with me daily, sang me to sleep when I was frightened and then, when she had a house of her own, she invited me to live with her. My first and second greatest gifts in this life were both bestowed by Collette. First the swing, second a home, but even more, I was initiated into the family immediately. Collette often called me "little sis," and I took to calling her, "Sissy."

Growing up in Saranac Lake was a like a treasured gift, one you wanted to appreciate and protect. I was allowed to attend school after a great debate between the doctor and my new family. My family wished to see me live a normal life. While they appreciated what my tutor was doing for me, they worried that I would become overly sullen if I weren't given a chance to mingle with children my own age. So I started school with great care and caution.

Like most young girls, I developed crushes on boys, although none of them was my knight. I excelled in my studies and swiftly rose to the head of my class. Because so many people were moving to Saranac Lake to take the mountain air cure, I was not secluded or alienated among my peers.

I was afraid of being shunned my first day of grade school, and while I was the only student wearing a cast, I was not the only child with consumption. Nearly everyone in the town was associated with the disease in one way or another. My fears quickly subsided and I had a fairly normal upbringing. Going to school was no cause for alarm as far as my condition went.

I was encouraged to take part in spelling bees and school plays. All these things boosted my confidence and filled me with a sense of belonging. Nana treated me as her own; when I did something wrong, I was scolded. I had chores and had to help in the kitchen during the canning season. Nana loved her canning. We made applesauce, preserves, pickles, and canned tomatoes with basil.

I was also praised when I detoured from my comfort zone and tried new things. I was terrified of water, but when Papa Joe surprised me with a canoe ride in one of his handmade boats, I said yes willingly. White knuckles on the side of the small craft, I soon released my fear and put my faith and confidence in the man who raised me.

I tackled things head on. When an arithmetic problem stumped me, I stayed after school for extra help. When I required a new brace, I dealt with it like the math problem. It was a nuisance but necessary in moving forward toward the answer.

I was treated with love and respect by my adopted family and thoroughly enjoyed my time in our home. The house was a large white Queen Anne-style abode. It boasted five bedrooms if you include the one off the den that was used for the cook. There was a single level cure porch downstairs as well as one that I preferred to use upstairs where I slept.

Our family consisted of me, Collette, Collette's mother, Christine, and Big Joe.

The first year was difficult because Miss Christine, who I had taken to calling Nana, had to endure numerous surgical procedures. When the pneumothorax appeared to be working, everyone sighed with relief, but after six months of enduring the procedure over and over again, additional surgeries were discussed.

First Dr. Trudeau brought up the plombage treatment, which inserted an inert substance into the pleural space in the diseased lung. The hope was if the diseased lobe of the lung collapsed on itself, it would heal more quickly than it would if left alone.

Second up for discussion was a lobectomy. In this case, Nana would have part of her diseased lobe removed. This was a serious surgical procedure that scared all of us. She was also a candidate for a pneumocotomy, which was a similar but more drastic procedure than the lobectomy. In the lobectomy procedure, only part of the lobe was removed, therefore allowing patients to have a better chance for optimal recovery. In the pneumocotomy, the whole lung would be removed, diminishing the opportunity for a full recovery.

There were other less invasive procedures, but Dr. Trudeau was less comfortable using them in Nana's case. He had performed numerous thoracoplasty procedures on other patients that involved the removal of several ribs in an effort to open up the chest and provide relief, but he didn't think her case was that dire, yet. He also talked with us about the use of shot bags. In this instance, the collarbones were weighed down with one ounce of shot per side, the amount of shot was increased by four or five ounces each week, until the patient had five pounds of weight on top of each lung. The additional weight thereby restricts the expenditure of the lungs, teaching correct breathing in the end. This procedure also allowed sick lungs an opportunity to heal under the weight.

Shot bags were a serious option for Nana. They would be far less invasive than other approaches but the doctor questioned the outcome. He felt certain a phrenicotomy would give her the best chance for optimal health. In this procedure, Nana's diseased lung would be permanently collapsed by crushing the phrenic nerve.

The surgery would paralyze the nerve supply to one side of the diaphragm, diminishing respiratory movements and decreasing the volume in the lung. As a result, the healing process could take place.

Luckily, for all of us, but especially for Nana, the phrenicotomy procedure worked. She needed a full month to get back on her feet, but she has been back on her feet ever since.

After that, Nana ran the household as a cure cottage and we had two patients residing with us most of the time. If I didn't hurry and beat them to the lavatory upstairs, I was late for school.

I forced myself out of bed, used the facility, and washed. Staring into my reflection in the bathroom mirror, I couldn't help but smile at myself and feel giddy. My posture was erect, more so than most as a result of my brace. My blond hair reached halfway down my back, and I was certain my hair was one of my finest assets. My eyes were blue, but not startling; I had freckles that ran across the bridge of my nose from soaking up the sun. I was pleased with what I saw and knew I was ready. In fact, I never felt more alive!

I wore my blue dress with the mutton sleeves, and had selected it purposefully for this occasion. I was leaving the grounds and going away to nursing school. It was an honor that I owed to Collette, for she instilled me with hope so many years ago when she received her nursing degree.

Collette had thought all hope was lost when her specimens came back active after nearly one year of being clear. But after twelve months she was as clear as a bell, was awarded a clean bill of health, and accepted into nursing school.

I would be going to St. Luke's Hospital Training School for Nurses in New York City. I would be a student in the third class to matriculate and looked forward to being back in the city where I was born.

"Is Collette here yet?" I yelled down the corridor to Nana.

"Not yet, dear, but she will be, don't you worry," Nana responded.

I took one last look in the mirror, grabbed my last suitcase, and took each step with precision as I made my way down the stairs. Waiting for me in the kitchen were Joe, Nana, and Dr. Trudeau. Will and Collette entered as I did.

"I don't suppose you'd want to come back here and work for me when you have your degree, would you?" the doctor asked.

"I don't know, doctor, I might be inclined to stay in the city." I felt a gigantic tug toward the city that teemed with life.

"Well, as long as you know you will always have a job here, if you want one," he said.

"Thank you, Dr. Trudeau, for the offer. Thank you for everything. You've been so kind and patient with me over the years and your research made me well. I will never forget that." I curtsied sincerely.

"We'd best be going," Will said, opening the door to the car that waited for me.

"Goodbye," Joe said, pulling me in for a hug.

"It's not goodbye, Joe, it's just until we see each other again. Thank you, for everything, Joe. I love you." I loved this man like a father and was sad to be leaving him.

"Come here, Amy," Nana said.

I went to her open arms and lay my head against her shoulder. For a moment my heart was heavy; leaving the people who had taken me in and become my family was the hardest thing I have ever faced emotionally.

"Thank you, Nana, you have been like a mother to me and for that I am grateful. I will be back for the holidays and until then, I will miss you all terribly," I said.

"Wait, let me get the Kodak box for a photograph." We posed together on the porch, side by side, as a family. Joe, Nana, Collette, Will, and myself. The only ones missing from this photograph were Beatrice and Steven, Collette and Will's children who were with Will's family for the week we would be away.

Nudging me forward, Collette took hold of my elbow with one hand and grabbed the basket carrying our lunch with the other. Then the three of us were off to the city.

CHAPTER 20

❧

NEW YORK CITY

Collette could not be contained. She hated being apart from her children, but she hadn't seen her brothers, Lucas, Daniel, and Joey in nearly two years. Daniel was interning for a prominent architectural firm where Lucas worked. Joey attended a prep school in the city, so he too was going to be there for the reunion.

"We're almost there," the driver informed us as we approached the beautifully appointed Plaza Hotel where we were meeting the men.

Collette took her powder puff from her clutch and swept it across her forehead, nose, and chin. Nerves had turned to excitement and she clapped her hands together like a schoolgirl. "Do I look all right?" she asked Will and me.

Will and I shared a chuckle. Collette was often so serious, that to see her giddy was a thrill.

"You look beautiful, darling, just beautiful," Will answered with great sincerity.

The driver pulled the car up to the hotel entrance and we unloaded our bags. My baggage was the most cumbersome, but tomorrow, I would check into my lodging so I only had to tote it for one afternoon.

The hotel was handsome indeed, warm-toned brick archways with iron gates at the entryway gave way to a lobby that was just as picturesque. If I hadn't just traveled here, I would be hard pressed to believe I was within the city limits. Large windows were adorned with gold jacquard drapes that puddled at the floor, rose plants and indoor trees were strategically placed to resemble a courtyard. An organist sat in the corner lulling the patrons into a relaxed state, while ladies with peacock plumes in their hats leisurely sauntered by, leaving behind the scent of the perfume that they were doused in. I felt an uncanny sense that I didn't belong here. I was not high society and never wished to be. I was uncomfortable and suddenly longed for home.

"There you are!" Lucas had seen us enter and came rushing to our side at once. He looked dapper in his perfectly fitting suit and highly polished shoes.

The older of the two redheaded men that followed caught my attention indeed.

"Lucas, Joey, Daniel!" Collette ran to her brothers, hugging them all at the same time.

"Joey, I can hardly believe it, you have to be six feet tall, and so handsome!" Collette exclaimed, taking in the sight of her youngest brother.

"Pardon me, where are my manners." Lucas stepped forward and introduced himself to me. I hadn't met the men because Collette always ventured to Rochester to visit them, they were busy with jobs and school, and I hadn't been given clearance to travel until recently.

"How do you do?" I asked while I took his hand, which he kissed, and curtsied.

"Pleased to finally meet you, Amy. We have heard so much about you," Lucas said, followed by Joey.

"I am Daniel, pleased to meet you, Amy." The gentleman before me was a man my age, his hair was auburn and his eyes hazel. I swooned and dropped my baggage.

"Oh, no." Will stepped to my side at once, holding me steady and gripping my bag.

"Are you okay? Amy, what's wrong?" Collette grew frantic at once. She always fretted over me and was not very happy that I was going to the city for school.

"I am fine, just a tad dizzy I think, due to the travel," I said, feeling embarrassed.

Daniel came to my side, grabbed my arm, and suggested we get something to eat and rest for a while before touring the city streets.

When he held my arm in the crook of his elbow, I knew immediately this was my knight. I wasn't searching for love, but knew without a doubt I had found it. He was articulate, charming, handsome, and courteous. He was also a student like myself.

After we were seated, the conversation bounced from life in the city to life in the mountains. I could barely focus on the conversation. I was love-struck, but not just with Daniel, our meal was otherworldly. The rich Italian fare paired fresh rolled gnocchi in a creamy sage sauce, mussels in a chunky tomato bath with herbs, fresh baked bread, and chocolate mousse for dessert. I was in heaven.

I felt revived after eating, but when I rose to pardon myself, I swooned once more. Collette accompanied me to the ladies room.

"I am not comfortable leaving you here, Amy. You nearly fainted, twice!" She furrowed her brows and stared intently into my eyes searching for answers.

"But I didn't and I am fine," I replied.

"What if you did and you were alone on the streets? The hooligans out there are just waiting to take advantage of someone like you."

"Someone like me? I am not a frail little lark, Collette. I can manage fine on my own," I said.

"Can you?" she asked.

"Stop treating me like a baby!" I raised my voice and realized that this was the first time we ever exchanged words that were less than pleasant. I appreciated the concern, but didn't want to be fawned over either.

"Fine." Collette stormed out of the bathroom and back to the table without waiting for me.

After I smoothed my hair and powdered my nose, I too went back to our party.

Sensing the tension between his sister and me, Daniel offered to show us around the city. First, we dropped our bags in our adjoining rooms upstairs in the hotel, then we proceeded with our tour.

"Collette tells me you lived here when you were young, do you remember where?" Daniel asked.

"It was over on Broadway, one of the high-rise buildings. I can't recall the address, but I would recognize the building. It had two lions guarding it, they had rings in their mouths and to a small child looked awfully fierce." I remember being afraid of the lions that guarded the entryway to our building.

"Broadway, what were you doing over there?" Daniel asked.

"My mother was an actress and my father her stage manager." Daniel and I walked ahead of our party, talking alongside one another as if it were the most natural thing in the world. He listened when I spoke of my family and expressed his condolences sincerely when he learned I had lost everyone in my life. I hadn't spoken so freely with a man before now and I didn't feel nervous at all. When others asked about my family, I quickly changed the subject, so why was I willing to discuss this with a complete stranger?

The afternoon flew by, and before I knew it, we were saying our goodbyes. The men had full schedules for the rest of the week so it was just Will, Collette, and I. The tension still hung like thick fog between us. I was tired of being treated like an invalid and wanted a chance to prove I was capable.

I understood why Collette would be worried, but I was not reckless, I was here to be a student of nursing and provide myself with a bright future.

We ate a small supper of bread and cheese in our room before retiring for the night.

When the morning came, my first thought was of Daniel. Imagine my delight when I went down for breakfast and found him in the dining room reading a newspaper.

"I was able to get the day off. I thought I might accompany you to your school and see that you get situated." He folded the paper and set it down on the side table.

I didn't know whether Collette planned this or not, but either way I was happy to have his company for another day.

CHAPTER 21

※

FINDING LOVE

The sisters at Saint Luke's Hospital Training for Nurses made it clear from the beginning what they expected from their students. Those of us in this classroom were the chosen few because our admission essays proved we were constitutionally strong young women who wanted to make a difference in the world. The sisters would not tolerate any shenanigans in their program. Anyone who fell below a B grade in any class would be put on detention immediately.

Nurses were once considered nothing more than domestic service people, but with the program set before me involving anatomy, physiology, biology, chemistry, and more, I quickly learned what a seriously skilled profession this was. Furthermore, nothing and no one could take my mind from my studies.

I spent my youth in search of answers. Why me, why was I spared when my entire family was not? I became philosophical and serious when searching for the greater meaning to my life. I was serious and studious, quiet, yet confident.

Two weeks into my courses, I learned why I was called to be a nurse. I was walking from St. Luke's nursing school to my humble apartment when I saw packs of children, orphans most likely, begging on the street corners. I counted the change in my pocket and walked to the vendor selling apples and oranges; I bought one dozen of each. I approached the ruffians and offered them the fruit. They didn't ask to be street urchins and beggars, it was their lot, just as tuberculosis was mine. The children ate the fruit greedily, apple peels, cores, seeds, and all. I noted the filthy condition of the children, witnessed the rot on their feet, the scabies patches on their skin. But it was the pair of siblings with splotches of red on their shirts who broke my heart, for I knew all too well what that splattered blood indicated.

I promised to be back tomorrow at the same time if they wanted more to eat.

The next day, the pair of siblings arrived, a few other children came as well, but for the most part the pack had run on to a different street corner.

I offered sandwiches to the kids and sat with them while they ate. I noticed how they wolfed down the food and assumed it was likely their only meal for the day.

The siblings were rather thin, but the whole group was filthy dirty and smelled rancid. My heart felt heavy watching them because I knew they were alone in the world like I had been at their age. Perhaps consumption was my good fortune. If I didn't have a kindly neighbor who took me in and looked after me, I would never have made it to the Sans for treatment. My father used to say, "Everything happens for a reason, darling girl," and in hindsight I think he was correct.

I told the children I was a nursing student and that I'd like to examine them the following afternoon at the clinic at St. Luke's. The only one that arrived was the little girl whose name was Carina. I asked about her brother, but she said he was resting.

"Is he feeling ill, Carina?" I asked.

"Yes, ma'am, I think he has the fever," she replied.

"Can you take me to him?" I asked.

"No," she replied without any further explanation.

"But I could help him," I told her.

Sister Mary Theresa saw the urchin and offered to give her a hot bath and warm bed for the night after her examination.

The child was teeming with head lice but refused the bath and bed. She only came for a meal, which we provided.

I wanted to follow her when she left but the sister grabbed my arm, "You have to earn her trust, Amy, that's all. She will come back tomorrow. You wait and see."

I spent my morning in classes learning the basics of pharmacology, followed by theory. After lunch, my afternoon was filled with a biology class and lab. My lab partner couldn't stand the sight of blood so the dissecting was up to me. I was careful when slicing my scalpel through the splayed frog's abdomen, then pulling back its skin with tweezers to get a good look at the inside. We would be tested next week on all the organs and I planned on getting an A.

The afternoon went by in a jiffy; my classmates wanted to share dinner together, but I needed to get to the clinic in case Carina came back. Sure enough, she entered quietly through the front door, wearing the same filthy clothing she had on the day before.

"Ahh, Carina, you have returned!" I approached her with a smile. "You must be hungry."

The little girl nodded, so I sat her down in an examination room and Sister Theresa brought her a heel of bread smothered with honey butter.

We were able to comb out the child's hair; it was snarled and clumped together, but the nits in her scalp needed removal. She had dried blood under her fingernails and the itching was nonstop. We had a special comb and ointment that worked wonders on the hair. We were hard pressed to get the child into a tub, but she did allow me to bathe her with a sponge. The grime filled my basin with murky brown water and I had to empty it several times.

While we waited for the doctor to attend to Carina, I asked about her brother.

"How is your brother today?" She wouldn't answer the question and looked like she wanted to run away.

The door opened and a young doctor entered. He wore a white doctor's coat over a handsome pin-striped shirt. He had a stethoscope dangling from his neck and a flashlight and two steel pens in his pocket.

"Hi, doctor, my name is Amy, I am a nursing student here," I introduced myself.

"Pleased to meet you, Amy, and who do we have here?" he asked.

"This is Carina. I met her a few days ago and offered to examine her." Carina evaded the doctor's eyes, and proceeded to cough into her dress, producing speckles of red that she tried to cover up.

"Let's take a look, shall we then?" The doctor had Carina take deep breaths; I noticed the scowl across his face when she obliged.

"Very good, then Carina. Amy, may I speak with you for a moment?"

We stepped into the hallway. "What do you know about this child?" he asked.

"I know she has a brother and that they are orphans. But the brother hasn't shown up for two days now. She always comes alone."

"I suspect she has the plague." I was immediately impressed by the doctor's diagnostic skills as well as his bedside manner.

"I suspect the same."

"You do? I thought you were just a student in your first year?" He wasn't being rude in any fashion, simply curious as to how I would make such an assessment.

"I am all too familiar with tuberculosis, I am afraid. I am concerned for her welfare, and that of her brother. I'm afraid he may be really sick, she says he has the fever."

"Okay. Let me think for a moment."

"She can stay here tonight; Sister Mary Theresa has a room ready and a meal prepared."

"That's very kind. But if the brother is out there, I doubt very much she will agree to stay."

The doctor was right. Carina left after she ate her fill; we wrapped a sandwich for her brother as well and hoped she would come back for further care. I couldn't stand to see the child go. I felt helpless and useless. My aim was to heal, not to send the frightened children back to whatever squalid living conditions they came from. If they only wanted food, they could go to a mission. I had to do something, I just didn't know what.

"Amy, pardon me, but you look troubled." The young doctor was handsome, and kind too.

"Just worried. I better head home. Doctor, thank you for seeing her."

"I hope you aren't walking home alone at this time of night?" he asked, concerned as it was after eight o'clock and was dark outside.

"If a small child can walk about the city alone, then surely I can," I responded.

"If you can wait a few minutes while I finish up, I can see you home."

"Oh, that's not necessary, really, I am not far."

"I insist." The doctor finished his notes and I stripped the examination tables and fit them with fresh linens. I cleaned the instruments and said goodnight to the attending sisters.

"After you," the doctor held the door for me, and we walked together into the city streets that were lit by the moon.

"Can I buy you a coffee or tea, perhaps?" he asked boldly.

"Oh. I suppose so." I was caught off guard, but would prefer his company to an empty room and studying.

We went to a tearoom and enjoyed pound cakes with apricot jam alongside steaming mugs of tea.

"So tell me, what brings you to New York City?" he asked.

"It's a long, long story, doctor."

"Please, call me Henry," he interrupted.

"Henry, it's a long story." It was indeed, and I wasn't comfortable discussing it with him yet.

"No pressure, just curious." He seemed to understand that I was holding back.

"The long and short of it is that from the time I was seven years old I have wanted to be a nurse. So here I am."

"How do you like it so far, the program you're in, I mean."

"Ask me after my first exam," I joked.

Our conversation flowed freely from here. As long as I didn't have to share my personal history with this man, I was willing to discuss all types of things. We were in the middle of discussing a nurse's role in the emergency room when Daniel walked into the tearoom with a striking woman on his arm. I shifted in my seat hoping he didn't see me, but it was too late. Our eyes locked, and he looked momentarily stunned.

"Why, Amy, it's grand to see you, how are your classes going?" he asked.

Henry stood up to introduce himself to Daniel, who introduced himself as Dan. He also introduced the woman he was with, saying she, Lana, was a business associate. But her eyes were like daggers, staking her claim on her date.

"Classes are fine, thank you for asking. How about you, how is the internship?"

"Internship?" the floozy asked, confused, "I thought you worked there, Danny?" she asked.

"I do work there, momentarily," he blushed, and I felt sorry for having embarrassed him. His date obviously thought he was more important than he was.

"Good to see you out and about, let's get together soon," he said to me before sitting down at a table across the room from us.

"Someone you know well?" Henry asked.

"Yes and no." I hated being evasive, but I didn't want to divulge my history. In fact, I was not surprised by how upset seeing Daniel with another woman made me. I pegged him as my knight, not hers.

I finished my tea and feigned an excuse that I was swamped with homework and needed to head home. In reality, I wanted to find Carina. I let the doctor walk me to my door. I went inside and turned on a light. I waited five minutes, grabbed a warmer sweater, and set back out. I walked right into Daniel.

"Where to?"

"Where to, yourself, where's your girlfriend, Lana?" I asked, as I put extra emphasis on the middle "a."

"She isn't my girlfriend, I can assure you," he replied.

"Well, assuming from the daggers she was giving me, she'd like to be." How was it that I spoke so candidly with this man?

"No, but really, it's late, where are you headed? I can walk you."

"Never mind, you'll just be like everyone else and tell me to go back inside." I had given up on finding Carina tonight and turned back toward my apartment.

"Whatever it is you're after, I can help you. No questions asked."

"Really, you'd do that for me?" I was impressed.

"Sure, why not."

"I'm just trying to find someone is all, a little girl who I have helped a few times. She's alone with her brother, and I'm worried about them."

"There are hundreds of thousands of orphans on these streets, Amy, you can't save them all."

"I can sure try, or at least die trying."

Daniel and I walked across town, listening to the city sounds; it was loud and raucous in some parts and downright peaceful in others.

"Do we know where we're headed? Or are we just looking aimlessly?" he teased.

"I want to go back to the place I first saw her. I can't imagine she would be too far from there, I am just a little turned around is all." I was having difficulty getting my bearings.

"We have company. Stay right beside me."

"Howdy." A group of three scraggly men approached us from behind. Daniel turned to face the men and pushed me behind him.

"You two seem to be on the wrong side of the tracks. You looking for something?" the tallest man in the trio asked, spitting tobacco at our feet.

"Just going about our own business is all," Daniel answered.

"Well, anything that happens on this side of town is my business, so tell me, what is a fine specimen such as yourself doing out at this time of night?" The stocky man smoking a cigarette circled me, and reached out to feel my tresses.

"Stop that," Daniel said, firmly and unafraid.

"We'll just be on our way," I said to the men.

The threesome had us cornered. The stocky man was pawing at me, grabbing at my clothes while the other two were provoking Daniel.

"You won't be going nowhere, son, not without a price. Now how about the pretty lady does us a favor and then you can be on your way." That the man insinuated I would stoop to such nasty and ludicrous behavior infuriated me, so I stepped forward and clocked him one right in the nose.

Daniel wasted no time and kicked the man to my right in the groin, bringing him to his knees. Then he punched the taller fellow with an uppercut to the chin. The man spun around and fell to the ground. But the fellow I punched was on him with punches to the gut and face. Daniel landed a strong one that sent the guy sailing.

"Let's get out of here." Daniel reached for my hand, and we ran for it.

When we got back to Broadway Street, I was out of breath and feeling labored. Running was not something I was used to, and I was sure we just ran three-quarters of a mile.

"Thank God you were with me, Daniel. Are you all right? The short man got you, didn't he?" His face was swelling, and he was also out of breath.

"Come in, let me take a look at that inside." I unlocked the door and led Daniel inside. I didn't care if the sisters saw me bring a man inside. Daniel was as close as family and I would be darned if I didn't at least owe him a towel and soap to clean up with. He was bleeding profusely from the gash on his eye.

"That is why everyone else warned you not to go out in the city at night. I was a fool. I just wanted to impress you. I am sorry, Amy. That could have gotten very ugly. I can't believe you clocked that guy though, I am impressed. Let me feel those muscles," he teased.

"But, Daniel, that's why I have to go back, every night if need be until I find Carina. She is so little and out there alone!"

I settled Daniel at my dining room table, which doubled as my desk. I moved my drawings from anatomy class and notes from theory to the bed.

"You need stitches. The cut above your eye is pretty deep."

"You gonna call your doctor friend?" he asked in a peculiar way.

"No, I don't need to call Henry, I am going to fix you up myself. I have everything I need right here."

"Henry, that's right. Henry, kind of a snobby name, don't you think?"

"Oh, stop it." I meant stop his fussing so I could stitch him smoothly, but he stopped talking all together. My hand was steady as ever thanks to years of practicing the art of being still. It took five stitches and he was closed up.

"That should do it, you were a good patient, didn't even flinch."

"It's not my first time getting stitches, but you have a good hand, the last lady wasn't as gentle." He sneered while telling me the story of his first stitches.

We were silent while I cleaned the supplies, then he spoke. "You know, most people would just pass them by, maybe throw them a penny or two," he remarked about the city's growing problem of orphans.

"Well, I couldn't do that, they need help. Besides, I'm not most people."

"It's a big city, you gonna help all the ruffians then?"

"You're making fun of me."

"No, I'm not. But speaking of fun, do you ever do anything for yourself?" he asked, with raised eyebrows.

"Why, yes, I am studying so that I may be a nurse," I gestured to my books that were stacked neatly beside my papers and pens.

"But that's to help others, what about you? What do you like to do for you?"

I couldn't answer that question because I didn't know.

He reached out for me then. I didn't know how to behave with a man so I stepped back. He took this to mean I was uninterested, so he made me promise not to go back out alone. Then he left.

I couldn't sleep at all that night. My mind was on the little girl and her brother, not to mention Daniel. I wanted to kiss him so badly. I hadn't been kissed by a man yet in my life and I was eager. I didn't mean to be coy, but I fear I was.

I also thought of Henry; he was so thoughtful and kind. I had two men on my mind when really I should be only focusing on my studies.

In the morning, a letter arrived from Nana and Joe, announcing they were coming for a visit in a few weekends. They hoped to spend time with me as well as the boys, Lucas, Daniel, and Joey. I could hardly wait to share the news with Daniel; I would find him after school today.

Instead, I was assigned a special task by the sisters to assist Henry at the hospital. He was caring for several children who had been diagnosed with tuberculosis and wanted my assistance with spica casting and pneumoplactys.

When he described the procedure to me, I stopped him short, "Henry, I know the procedure, I have seen it done a dozen times or more."

Henry looked confused and surprised. "Wonderful, then. Excellent. As long as you know what's in store, then let's get on with it." He wheeled a cart with supplies toward me, and we began seeing patients. At the end of the day, Henry was mystified.

"There is something about you, Amy. What aren't you telling me?" he asked.

"I have spent a lifetime around patients with TB, I am one."

"What?"

I explained my situation, my life at the Sans, my clear specimens, all of it. I left out the part about my family. He didn't need to know that. All this doctor needed to know was that I was capable of helping anyone I could with this god-awful disease.

"It's been a long day, but I wondered if you'd like to grab a quick bite. Someplace on the way home," he asked.

"Golly. I really shouldn't, I have to study for my exam tomorrow. Another time?"

"I understand." He thought I was turning him down, just like Daniel.

"On second thought, yes, I need to eat, before I fall down," I laughed.

He looked relieved and once more left only to finish his notes and we were off. Dinner was casual; we had soup and sandwiches, nothing more. A turkey sandwich never tasted so good. It was a long, productive day. I worried about the patients we attended earlier and said so to Henry.

"I will check in on them first thing in the morning. If any problems arise tonight, the nurse will ring me."

Henry told me that his father was a family practitioner and that he'd wanted to be a doctor for as long as he could remember. He was from Chester County, so studying and working in New York was not a far leap for him. I shared with him stories from the Sans, what is was like growing up there among so many people who were ill.

"It must have been sad," he stated.

"At times it was, when someone passed away, or someone wasn't faring well. But you know, living in Saranac Lake allowed me to be normal. No one shunned me for being ill. I was allowed to eat in restaurants with my family, or go into any shop I chose. I attended school and church like everybody else. I know there are towns that don't allow anyone who has active consumption to set a foot in the doorway."

"It's true. My town was and still is that way. There is still so much we don't know about the disease. Yes, the research is ongoing and although we can diagnose it now, there is no cure, so people are afraid."

Henry was interested in my symptoms for spinal TB and asked what other types of cases I had seen. He was an astute listener and made for good company.

"I don't wish to be too forward, but I have tickets to the opera on Friday night. I'd be honored to take you, if you wish to go with me that is?" he looked nervously at me.

"Golly. I have never been to an opera. I am not sure I have anything appropriate to wear."

"Is that a yes, then?" he asked.

"That's a yes, but I may be a little underdressed."

Friday came too quickly, and I hardly had time to assemble an appropriate outfit for my date. I had one gown that would have to suffice. It was peach with mutton sleeves, had a buttoned brocade bodice that opened ever so slightly, showcasing my pearl necklace. The pearls were a gift from Nana on my sixteenth birthday. I wore pearl studs in my ears and swept my cheeks with a dusty pink blusher.

My bangs were long enough to braid and sweep around my head like a halo. The rest I knotted at the nape of my neck and for a final touch, I held the knot together with a tortoise shell comb.

Henry arrived at exactly six p.m. and we were off to have dinner at the infamous Delmonico's before the performance at The Metropolitan Opera House. The evening's performance was featuring Nellie Melba, a soprano born in Australia who moved to Paris to complete her training. We ate meatloaf and Italian beans smothered in garlic. I allowed myself one glass of wine and feared if I ate too much, I would bust out of my lumbar brace. It was already crushing me as it was.

When we arrived at The Met, I immediately felt self-conscious. I was severely underdressed and felt embarrassed for both myself and Henry.

Women were dripping in pearls; they wore diamond tiaras, silk gloves, and had trains trailing their gowns. The gowns were of chiffon, silk, taffeta, and rich velvet. In comparison, my peach ensemble was dowdy and unremarkable.

Sensing my discomfort and distress, Henry quickly remarked at what a spectacle the women at The Met were. We weren't here to see them after all, he quipped. We were seated in red velvet chairs. I sucked in my breath, for never in my life had I been in such an awe-inspiring atmosphere.

When Nellie was introduced and began performing, I was moved beyond measure. Each lilt of a note, each measure as she held it, was nothing if not breathtaking. During the intermission, I walked around while Henry went to fetch drinks. I couldn't help but reminisce about my mother, the way she sang around the house. I never did see her perform, and that caused me great pain.

Strolling through The Met, I took in the sights and sounds. I walked from the crowds of people toward a back hallway. Before me, framed among the great operatic acts of New York was a series of photographs. One was an image of a woman who I was sure was my mother. Beside her was an astute gentleman, not comfortable with the limelight, my father.

How could it be, was it a sign of some sort from them? I could not hold back the tears, they just came. I ran from the hallway and went to gather myself. I stood in line for the ladies room, trying to remain calm and not attract attention to myself.

"Is this your first time at The Met, dear?" the woman in line behind me asked.

"Why yes, it is," I answered.

"Every first timer cries, dear, here," she handed me a hanky she had folded in her sleeve. I took it and dabbed my eyes.

"Amy? Amy, is that you?" I turned from the line and saw Daniel.

"What on earth are you doing here?" I asked surprised to see him and embarrassed that I was crying like a child.

"Never mind what I'm doing here, what's wrong?"

"First timer," the lady with the hanky remarked, having overheard Daniel.

"I don't get the feeling you're crying just because of Nellie. You're crying because you're sad."

No sooner had he said the words than the light flickered announcing the end of the intermission. Henry was by my side; he had no luck getting drinks due to the long lines and was awfully apologetic.

"Nice to see you, Dan, is it?"

"You as well. Amy, do take care," Daniel said, leaving me to wonder who he was with.

"Are you all right?" Henry asked, noting my tears.

"First-time tears, that's all."

"Yes, the first time is indeed remarkable."

When the show was over, I wished desperately to walk the corridors in search of more photographic evidence of my mother. I wanted to see newspaper clippings, anything to tell me what I missed. I was heartsick. Henry dropped me at home, kissed my hand like a true gentleman, and bid me goodnight. I was undressing when the door chime rang. Odd, I thought, I wondered if Henry left something by mistake.

"Just a moment," I hollered. I put on a robe and opened the door, leaving the chain lock intact.

Only it wasn't Henry, it was Daniel.

"May I come in?" he asked.

"I don't think the sisters would allow it."

– 203 –

"I don't care what the sisters allow, do you?"

I opened the door, but told him to be quiet. I didn't want to alert anyone that I had a gentleman caller. He took in the sight of me and at once pulled me close. I felt at home in his arms. My head nestled safely in the crook of his neck; I yearned for him deeply. His scent was masculine, yet I also detected balsam or pine. Yes, pine soap that was it. He began kissing my neck, then my chest. His fingers were in my hair, undoing my carefully knotted bun and braids.

"You're beautiful," he said, taking me in.

"You're a liar," I responded.

"Why were you crying?" he asked, in between his kisses.

"I don't want to talk about it."

"Okay, then let's not talk." He loosened the tie around my robe, and I let it fall to the ground. I stood before him, naked except for the cumbersome brace.

Instead of remarking on the brace, he adeptly began to remove it, starting with the truss buckle, resembling a corset, which was fastened at my sides. One by one, he unhitched the buckles and took my brace off, gently putting it aside.

"Does it bother you?" I asked.

"Bother me? Why would it bother me, it's a part of you."

"But you didn't expect it, did you. I don't want you to pity me."

"Pity? Never," he said, as he continued to undress me.

"Good," I said moving closer to him. I was not this type of woman. I was a virgin, had never even kissed a man before Daniel, yet here he was in my room, beside my bed. I was naked, but not self-conscious. This man admired me and regaled me with praise.

"So beautiful," he said once more as he lie me down, his hand instinctively beneath my head. He was careful, practiced I supposed, and gentle. His touch was electric; the current sent through my body was indescribable, I wanted him more than

I wanted anything. I grew moist between my legs and felt him growing with need as well. He made love to me fully and wholly many times throughout the night. I was a woman now, and I had no regrets, for this was my knight in shining armor who had come for me at last.

I fell into a sleep so deep and tranquil that I did not hear him when he got up to make coffee that morning. I did, however, hear a knock at my door. Startled, I saw that it was eight a.m. and wondered who would be at my door on a Saturday morning. I didn't want to get it, but in case it was news of Carina, I needed to. I shushed Daniel and pulled on my robe. I supported myself as I rose carefully. I was quite surprised to see the sisters looking cross when I opened the door.

"Amy, do you have a visitor?" They did not beat around the bush at all, simply came out with it and asked.

"Why, what do you mean?" Fear took over, if they found out Daniel was here I could lose my place as a student. All my merit and hard work would be for naught. If I lied, I could never look them in the eyes again.

"Do you have a gentleman caller?" Sister Theresa repeated the question.

"I do, sister."

Daniel was up and dressed, he came to the door and opened it wide.

"How do you do, sisters? I am Daniel Lyndon. Amy's husband."

I gulped back my surprise and tried not to look too astonished.

"Amy, is this true?"

"Yes, this is my husband." My voice cracked when I said the word husband.

"Where is your ring?" Sister Mary asked.

"We were only just wed, sister, the rings are still being engraved."

"I see. We shall need to see your certificate of marriage then.

As you know we don't allow any men in the apartments that aren't family."

"Yes, ma'am, sister," I stumbled with my words.

Daniel came up beside me looking worried, "But, dearest, I was having it framed for you. It is at the frame shop now. It was part of my wedding gift."

"Oh! That was so kind." I wrapped my arms around Daniel in honest appreciation for something fabricated.

"I can bring it to you as soon as I get it back, will that suffice?" I asked the sisters.

"Very well." The sisters left, and we closed the door. I lay down because I was laughing so hard.

"What's so funny?" Daniel asked, leaning into me, he wanted to make love again.

"What are we going to do now?" I didn't know whether to laugh or cry. The whole thing was so out of character for me.

"Get married," he said, while placing gentle kisses on my neck.

"You can't be serious?"

"Why not?"

"Why, because we hardly know each other, that's why not."

"We know each other well enough. I think I fell for you the moment I first saw you at the Plaza Hotel."

"Truthfully?" I asked, eager for his answer.

"Truthfully," he replied.

CHAPTER 22

❦

WEDDING BELLS

I became Mrs. Daniel Lyndon overnight. The whirlwind wedding was attended by Lucas, who acted as his brother's best man, and his wife, Esther, who sponsored me. Joey was there as well and acted as an additional groomsman. The brothers appeared genuinely happy for us and said as much numerous times. I wore my peach gown and put baby's breath in my hair. I had a natural glow so that I didn't need to apply any blusher. Did I love this man? I did, indeed, but did I love him enough to marry him? We only just met, yet I have heard about him every day since my arrival at the Sans. I suddenly wondered how I was going to explain this to Henry. He was so kind to me, and I think his interest was more than platonic. Oh dear, that would have to be handled delicately.

All I wanted to think about for now was my husband, and getting him back in my bed. I never knew what I was missing all these years. Love has a language all its own; it's a form of expression that needs no words to be understood. Daniel and I made excellent lovers. We fit together perfectly and knew precisely how to please each other. I learned more about anatomy and physiology with my husband in a few short days than I would all year. After we consummated our marriage, we talked about our family.

"How do we tell them?" I asked.

"We just tell them. Mother and Big Joe will be here next weekend and we just tell them. Either they will be happy or they won't, but that doesn't change things with us, does it?"

"Should it?" I asked in reply.

"Would you believe me if I said I had never been with another woman before?"

"Hardly."

"Well, it's the truth. Shows how well you know your husband," he laughed.

"Really? I find that hard to believe. I've seen women fall all over you, take the blond from the tea lounge, for example."

"I swear it, you are my first, and you will be my only." With that admission, we made love once more. I suddenly glimpsed a future with children of my own. However, that future wasn't in the city, it was in the mountains.

"Last night, when I was crying?"

"Yes, you didn't want to talk about it."

"Well, now I do."

"Okay."

"I saw a photograph of my parents at The Met. All of the 'could have beens' suddenly flashed before my eyes. I was one of five children. I was the only one in the whole household that survived." I was overcome with emotion. The realization I was married, coupled with the loneliness I felt for my family was unbearable.

"I am your family now, Amy. We will have children of our own, if that's what you want?"

No one ever asked me what I wanted. I was always told how to walk so I didn't hurt my spine, how to study so I could grow up and go to school, how to eat to stay healthy. This was the first time anyone had ever inquired to what I wanted.

"It is what I want, Daniel, it's just you are the first person who has ever asked."

"Tell me then, what does your true heart desire?"

"My true heart is conflicted. I am sad and yet so grateful. Why did I live when no one else in my family did? How did I find you? How did I get so lucky?"

"I am the lucky one, perhaps you survived because I needed you?" he asked.

Our love caught us unaware. We were smitten with one another and our time in bed. My classes couldn't go by fast enough, nor could Daniel's days spent sketching and touring the city with his big brother. I beat him home most nights and started dinner. I remembered the succulent meals Nana prepared. The time she spent pounding the chicken, or braising a roast beef to make it more tender. I tried to emulate her dishes, but my potato mash was never as creamy and soups never as flavorful. It became the running joke between Daniel and me. We always had a backup plan for dinner in case my latest experiment failed. My husband was actually quite talented in the kitchen, he had spent a lot of time alongside his nanny, Quinn, who became his step-mother. Quinn was a culinary whiz, able to make sumptuous dishes with the simplest of ingredients. She would hand roll a flour and egg mix for raviolis stuffed with ricotta, then dress them with a simple sage cream sauce. Or she would stew vegetables and ladle them over a roast chicken. Simple, yet elegant and divine. Daniel quickly became the chef in our apartment. He was very happy when he cooked and even began to discuss it as a career.

"You know, I could open my own restaurant," he said one night after presenting me with a fig- and hazelnut-encrusted pork loin wrapped in bacon.

"You're not kidding. This is amazing, Daniel, simply divine. You have a gift."

"What should I make for Mother and Joe? They will be here in two days," the inflection in his voice giving away his excitement.

His life was interesting and divided like mine. He lost two of his siblings at a young age and was kept apart from his mother and one remaining sister growing up. He missed growing up with his true mother and took to writing her regularly so that they developed a relationship through their correspondence.

When Nana was cleared for several years, she decided to stay put in Saranac Lake. It had become her home and she never wanted to leave it, or her lover, Joe. Daniel wasn't given allowance to visit her because his father was afraid of contagion. Instead, once a year she took a carriage, or car as time advanced, to Pittsford. She stayed in a hotel and met her boys for lunch and afternoons in the park.

As Daniel became his own man, it was up to him to decide how he spent his time and he had a mind to go to Saranac Lake and see it in all its glory. The way it was described to him was nothing short of majestic.

"Anything you make will be appreciated. Just remember, your mother and Joe mostly dine on proteins, so I would stay away from pastas and sweets. How about your veal meatloaf? Or your peach chicken?"

"Perhaps the veal. I have a new recipe to try, it's not too rich, but I think they will enjoy it."

"Are you nervous? Should we have told them in a letter?"

"No, I am not nervous. They will see the love we have for each other and be happy for us. I know it."

"How will they understand that we met and fell in love, then married within a week?"

"That's the nature of love, I suppose. I just knew; one look at you as you hauled your luggage into the hotel with my sister. I was smitten. I wanted you for my wife right then."

"But you didn't know me, or anything about me."

"I didn't need to; here you were, traveling to New York to study and become a nurse. The courage that takes is astounding. Then I saw you…that little rump of yours…."

I smacked Daniel with a dish towel; he loved to tease me about my curvaceous rump. I was quite pleased with it myself, considering how thin I had always been. With Daniel's cooking, I was packing on weight around my middle too.

"You better be careful or you'll have yourself a plump wife in no time."

"The plumper the wife, the more to hold and love," he said with a huge grin, offsetting his dimples.

That evening was no different; we ate, took care of the dishes, and studied side by side. Daniel quizzed me on my anatomy, and I looked over his sketches for buildings. Then we fell into bed, rolling around the sheets and loving one another until we were spent. The following two days passed by in a hurry; I aced my exam and Daniel had a bid accepted for a project. We had much to celebrate aside from the visit from our family. When the carriage carrying Nana and Joe finally arrived, Daniel hopped over the curb first and held out his hand for Nana who climbed down with more caution.

"Mother!" Daniel beamed at his mother and encircled her in a large hug, twirling her in his arms so that her skirt left the ground. He put her down and turned to Joe. "Sir," he reached for a hand shake, but Joe pulled him in for a hug as well.

Then it was my turn to embrace my loved ones. I had missed these two people more than I thought possible. They were the constant in my topsy-turvy life.

"Nana, Joe, I have missed you!" I hugged them both and stood back to have a look at them. Nana's weight had dropped once more, and while Joe looked happy to see us, I could tell he was concerned about something.

"Look at the pair of you, how is everything in New York?" they asked.

"Oh New York is full of surprises," Daniel answered.

We took their baggage to the hotel lobby and checked them with the bellman. Then we strolled along Park Avenue, taking in the sights that made up this remarkable city. Each parcel of space on the city's streets was negotiated by either the socialites who walked with their poodles and pugs trailing behind them, or the working class whose quick strides dictated their importance. Fruit vendors and flower stands stood at every corner selling their finest assortments. Street sweepers and bootblacks were at work and the city hummed along like a well-rehearsed orchestra.

"Are you hungry?" Daniel asked, after we had taken in the sights for nearly an hour.

"Your son has become quite the chef!" I announced.

"So have the two of you been able to spend some time together then?" they asked, unaware of just how much time we'd spent together.

"Some," Daniel answered with a smirk before grabbing my hand and kissing it.

"I can't stand it for another minute. Mother, Joe, we have news. Amy and I are married." Nana sat down she was so overcome with emotion and Joe slapped his back with congratulations.

"Married? What do you mean you're married, when? How?" Nana asked.

"We met, fell in love, went to the town court, said our I do's and became wed." Daniel, never one to mince words, had a way of simplifying things and laying them out flat so everyone could see the clarity in his way of thinking.

"My heavens, darlings, congratulations are in order. Amy, didn't you want a wedding in a chapel?" she asked me with a look of concern.

"Not really, Nana, I just wanted to be with Daniel, the rest didn't matter."

"But it mattered to me," she said. "I would have had a fine reception for you, if I knew."

"Don't be mad now, Mother, we are two young lovers and we couldn't wait. I am sure you can understand." He winked at Joe, who couldn't hide his smirk.

"I am not mad, not at all. I couldn't be happier for the pair of you. You deserve one another, in fact, I don't know why I didn't think of matching you two up sooner. I just wish I could have been there."

"I would have liked to give you away," Joe said.

"Well, who's to say we can't have a proper ceremony still?" Daniel asked.

"Really, Daniel, would you want that?" I asked with excitement in my voice.

"Surely. I'd love to have our wedding night all over again, and maybe even take a proper honeymoon," he wiggled his eyebrows up and down and laughed out loud.

"Could we have it in Saranac Lake? So that Dr. Trudeau and his family, and all our friends, could come witness the event?"

"That sounds swell to me," Daniel answered. We hugged and kissed in front of Nana and Joe, the four of us, my family.

Lucas and his wife joined us, and over a meal of veal shanks, Burgundy mushrooms, and sliced tomatoes, we discussed the wedding plans. I didn't want to tax Nana with the arrangements because I was aware she wasn't one hundred percent well. She appeared symptomatic again.

"Nana, we'll be home for the holidays, perhaps we can have a small ceremony at the chapel then. The family will want to be together to celebrate the Thanksgiving holidays anyway. Let's keep it simple, a small ceremony with family and friends."

"It sounds lovely. I can have Patty Marshall make the cake and Julie Simmons will do the flowers."

"Perfect, I'll leave it in your capable hands, nothing too fancy though, okay, Nana?"

"Understood, you want it to be simple and elegant. It will be lovely."

The weekend went by too quickly; I had a moment with Joe alone and asked about Nana. He said she had been ill recently, and that's when she lost her weight. I noted that she sat more than she stood and that she tired very easily. I hadn't seen her like this since before her pneumothorax and my concern grew.

I would talk to Henry about this. I had to speak to Henry about a few things actually.

CHAPTER 23

⚜️

DELICATE MATTERS

I ducked into the hospital between classes to steal Henry for a moment. When he saw me enter, his eyes widened and he smiled. He scribbled something on his notepaper, clicked his pen, stowed it away in his shirt pocket and came toward me.

"Amy, what brings you here this afternoon? I am delighted to see you," he leaned toward me and kissed my cheek.

"Why thank you, doctor. I needed to speak with you about a few things actually," I said.

"Is that one of them?" he asked, gesturing toward my simple wedding band. Daniel and I purchased very simple and matching gold bands.

"Yes, it is. I am sorry, Henry. I wasn't leading you on, I was enjoying our time together, but Daniel is someone from my past and we sort of fell in love overnight. I know it's hard to believe, but it's the truth."

"I am happy for you, Amy, truly I am. Dan is a fine man and I wish you a lifetime of happiness."

That went better than I expected. Henry was letting me off the hook with more ease than I deserved.

"There is something else. My Nana, well she's not really my Nana, but regardless, she is TB positive. She had a collapsed lung ten years ago and has been doing remarkably well until recently."

"It's hard for me to comment or assess unless I see her. Pneumothoractic procedures usually work long term in healing the diseased lung. But I have seen numerous patients who rebound after a period of time and then require a lobectomy."

"Goodness. That's a rather serious procedure," I remarked, thinking of what a lobectomy required.

"It is, but I know several surgeons who have done this with great success rates."

I didn't want Nana to be a statistic, so I thanked Henry, then inquired if Carina had showed herself again. She had not. I left the hospital with a heavy heart. When I told my husband what Henry thought about Nana, he suggested we ring Collette. They had a telephone service now and he was more than happy to pay for the call.

"Hello?" Collette answered.

"Collette, is that you? It's Amy!" I missed her so much at this precise moment and worried she was still mad at me for raising my voice to her.

"Amy, is everything all right?" she was worried.

"Better than all right. I have exciting news! Daniel and I got married!" I yelled my news into the receiver. I detailed our marriage, leaving nothing out, for Collette was the one person I could speak to about intimate matters. She asked about my nursing courses and I told her I was getting As in everything but statistics. Then we discussed Nana. I told her what Henry thought and she said that Dr. Trudeau concurred. Nana simply did not want to endure another risky procedure. She was content to live out her days peacefully at the Lake, but wanted no part in another surgery. She was adamant about this. Now I understood why the wedding was so important to her.

Nana corresponded regularly with me over the fall, detailing the plans for the wedding she would orchestrate. I reminded her to keep it small and simple, but every time we spoke, the list had grown to include more friends and relatives. I was more than happy to let Nana plan the event however she chose. I hated thinking this way at all, but it did occur to me that the wedding would provide her an opportunity to see her beloved family, which was spread out across the state of New York, one last time.

Collette rang occasionally to discuss Nana's deteriorating condition. She used a wheelchair to get around now and reserved her energy for wedding planning. Collette took care of the home and the two patients who resided there. It was taxing for her, because she had her own family to take care of; luckily Will was a kind and noble man. He stepped up to help whenever necessary. As he had seen in the past with other patients at the Sanitarium, too much exertion could reignite the active disease and he certainly didn't wish this for his wife.

I wondered what it would be like to have children; did Daniel desire them like I did? Would it be safe for me to bear them, carry them for a full nine months? I hadn't thought of the physical aspect until now. Daniel and I made love daily and although my courses came regularly, perhaps we had better take proper measures to prevent a pregnancy.

"Daniel," I said to him one night as we lay side by side in bed.

"Yes, dearest, what's on your mind?"

"Babies."

"Babies?"

"Yes, do you want them?" I asked.

"Why, I suppose I do, if they take after their mother. Do you?"

"I have always wanted precisely four children. Two boys, born first, two years apart. Followed by two girls, born two years apart. But, Daniel, now I am afraid," I admitted.

He rolled to face me. "What are you afraid of?"

"I am afraid I won't be able to carry them. It would break my heart if I couldn't. I don't want to be selfish in any way, but Daniel, what if they disabled me? What if my vertebrae separate and I become disfigured? Then I won't be able to care for them and that would leave you to care for all of us." My dreams of being a mother were quickly dissolving before my eyes.

"I hadn't thought about that, really. I guess that was ignorant of me. I hadn't considered your situation entirely and for that I am truly sorry."

"What should we do? We can find pleasure other ways."

"Yes, I suppose we can, but why not talk to a doctor about this instead of worrying about it for no reason?"

"Will you come with me?"

"Of course I will."

The appointment was scheduled for the following week and until then we focused on our studies and spent our time happy as newlyweds. I spent more and more time assisting Henry in the hospital with his TB patients and Daniel spent more time on assignment with his brother, so the week went by rather quickly. We rarely saw Joey due to his grueling school schedule.

There was no sign of Carina and her brother, and I conjured up the worst images about them in my mind. I thought of them suffering side by side in a hayloft somewhere, or worse, dead, bodies exposed to the elements, including hawks and rats that would nibble away at them like a dog with a bone. I talked to my husband about this and he understood why I was so concerned. I would have been alone on the streets if not for my kind neighbor.

"We'll keep looking for them, in the daylight though, dearest. I don't want any trouble like last time."

"Promise?" I asked him.

"Cross my heart. We can start this weekend, in the Five Points. It's not a pretty section of the city and I hate imagining you there, but my guess is the kids are there." Daniel hated the thought of youngsters alone as much as I did. He was not only my knight, but would be theirs too, if we could find them.

The day for the appointment came. Daniel and I walked the short distance to the doctor's office and enjoyed our afternoon together.

"Do you know what I love the most about you, Amy?"

"My fat rump?" I teased.

"No. Although I do fancy that. I love that you don't fret. You are a woman who takes action. You never whine or complain; you simply live. I admire it. I just wanted you to know," he squeezed my hand tighter, causing me to think.

"Don't put me on a pedestal, Daniel, that's a dangerous place to be."

"Why, I am afraid it's too late, you are already there. Pedestal or no pedestal, you have my highest esteem."

I wondered why Daniel was telling me this now. Was he afraid of the news we were about to receive or was he just a man in love, lavishing me with praise?

A nurse showed us into an examination room where I undressed down to my birthday suit. Daniel held my brace carefully and grimaced at the thought of another man looking at my womanly parts. He paced the small room, wearing a trail in the hard plank floors.

"Settle down, dear." I had to laugh at my husband.

"But, Amy, this man is about to put his hands on you, I just can't allow it. I'm just not sure I agree it is okay." I laughed out loud, but then the door opened, and a grandfatherly figure walked in.

"What's so funny?" he asked.

"Oh, my husband is just nervous about the exam."

He looked at my husband, whose face was flush with embarrassment and asked him to wait outside. Daniel did not hesitate for one second. He was out the door and the doctor and I had ourselves a good chuckle. He proceeded with the examination and asked me how far along I was.

"Oh, I'm not pregnant yet, doctor, I am just concerned about becoming pregnant. As it says in my file, I have had spinal tuberculosis."

"I see." The doctor helped me sit up and reviewed my file.

"Well, I don't know how to tell you this, but you already are pregnant. I would guess about six weeks. You are very tender, and besides that, you have a glow. I can do a urine screen to be sure if you wish, but I am always right."

"Goodness. I don't know whether to laugh or cry." Daniel had foreseen this somehow. That's why he talked about taking action, not complaining, just accepting a situation and making the best of it.

"Well, there are several mindsets when it comes to pregnancy and TB. Some doctors believe that pregnancy is actually beneficial to the woman during this time. It's thought that the expansion of the abdomen can collapse any open cavities, and promote healing. In other words, as the baby grows and pressure is applied to your abdomen, TB cavities close. Now, having said that, I am not inclined to think along these lines. I worry about reactivation for you, because you are my primary patient. I also worry about the progression and transference of the disease to the unborn child."

"What are my options, doctor?" I sat stunned. I had to close my eyes for a moment and consider everything he said.

"Well, you can carry on with the pregnancy and take bed rest. I would monitor you very closely for hepatoxicity, which is liver damage. I would have a pediatrician follow you to term to ensure the health of the baby. We want to make sure the fetus is not affected via the umbilical vein. However, because you aren't active currently, I feel the baby would be safe. It's you I worry about."

"Goodness."

"The other option is to have an abortion. You can terminate the pregnancy and use methods of birth control moving forward."

"Okay, doctor. Thank you for explaining it all to me. I'd like to tell my husband alone tonight, so please don't say anything."

Daniel was shown back in to the room and helped me into my brace. I erased the fact I was pregnant momentarily from my mind so that I could spend the afternoon with the love of my life without any worries.

The following week I spoke to my dear friend, Henry, about this delicate matter. He had a friend who could help me to terminate the pregnancy. I never disclosed the information to Daniel because I knew it would break his heart. I wished to spare him that at least. The thought of an abortion tore me up, but I was fighting for my own life, I didn't want to become disabled and for the very first time in my life, I thought of myself first.

On the morning of my procedure, I told Daniel I had to leave early for a study group. I rose and kissed him goodbye, giving him no reason to be concerned or question where I was going. I went to the hospital instead, where Henry was waiting for me. Henry understood the validity of a termination because he had vast medical knowledge and had seen numerous disabled, disfigured patients in massive amounts of pain. He didn't judge or question my decision, only the fact I refused to tell my husband.

I was stripped down and put into a mint green hospital gown, then my feet were put into stirrups. It was explained that I would be doused with chloroform and become unconscious.

"I'll be right beside you the whole time," Henry said, then nodded to the anesthesiologist and physician who were about to perform the procedure.

When I woke, I was exceedingly weak and groggy. It was difficult to focus, but I felt certain Daniel was with me.

"Amy, Amy, can you hear me?" Daniel spoke.

"Daniel!" I cried out to my husband.

"Yes, it's me. Henry called me. We almost lost you," the tone in his voice told me how frightened he was.

"I don't understand," I questioned what happened through a foggy haze.

Henry approached my bedside and told me the procedure had not gone well. I lost a great deal of blood and they weren't able to terminate the pregnancy.

"You'll stay at the hospital until you regain your strength. I'll check in on you later."

I was left alone with Daniel, he had tears in his eyes and I was terrified he would never speak to me again.

"Tell me what happened," he was gentle and loving, not mad.

"I didn't want you to suffer. I never wanted you to know."

"But you're my wife, I need to know. We are in this together now, Amy, don't you understand that?"

"I am scared, Daniel." I closed my eyes and let the tears stream down my cheeks. I was frightened.

"We can be scared together. We are a team, I am your knight, remember?"

I was sent home two days later. Daniel never left my side; he slept on a cot beside me, waking when I needed to use the john and helping me back and forth. I was still pregnant, still afraid of carrying a baby to term, becoming disabled and forcing Daniel into caring for us. He assured me he wanted nothing more than to care for us, and that he wanted a child more than anything.

I phoned Collette and told her to expand the seams in my dress because I was expecting. Her response was cautious. She knew all too well what this meant.

"Come home, Amy. We can take care of you while you're on bed rest. Daniel can visit on the weekends."

"He wants me to stay here, he wants to look after me himself. How can I deny him that after what I did before?"

"Perhaps I can come there for a spell?"

"That would be nice."

"What about your classes? Are you withdrawing for the semester?"

"I have to. I thought I would be dreadfully disappointed in myself, but you know, I have learned that life happens. This baby happened for a reason and my training can wait. Family is far more important."

"We all make sacrifices, you know that better than most. Keeping you and the baby safe is top priority now," Collette agreed.

"What about the wedding? What do we tell Nana?"

"I am worried about her; the wedding plans are sustaining her, Amy. She is not doing well, I am afraid." I heard the catch in her voice as she choked back tears.

"I am certain my doctor will allow me one weekend away, particularly if he knows I am under a doctor's care while there. Dr. Trudeau will look in on me if necessary, won't he?"

"Of course he will."

"Just think, in a few months, I will be home. We'll have a grand wedding, even if I am supposed to be on bed rest. I can take my vows in a chair and rest while the guests are milling about. This is really for Nana anyway."

"I can't wait to see you, and your baby. Do you think it's a girl?"

"I think it's a boy, who I shall name Daniel Edward Lyndon. He will have red hair like his father and be brilliant like him as well." We laughed and talked about flowers for the wedding before saying our goodbyes. Nana wanted bouquets with roses, green fern leaves, and baby's breath. I was content to go along with whatever she chose. I felt quite well and was more frustrated that I was on bed rest than anything else.

Daniel came and went as usual; he loved me at night, fearful at first of hurting the baby. The doctor assured us we did not need to abstain from sexual intercourse during my bed rest; I think because he knew it was my only entertainment all day long.

As a child, I dreamed of my future while taking my rest, now I dreamed of the past that led me here. How was I lucky enough to have this man beside me? Our dreams for a healthy family had to come true, they just had to. I was optimistic like the doctor told me to be, and for now, that was the only power I held.

Soon it was time to travel to Saranac Lake for our second wedding ceremony. We were surrounded by friends and family leading up to the event, making for a few chaotic, but nonetheless fun, days. Our arrival at the house was a blessing; Nana rose to the occasion, putting herself and her guests at the forefront of her mind, easing her pain and welcoming this time with loved ones. Nana's sister and her entire family arrived from Skaneateles; they were among the lucky few who remained untouched by consumption. Nana's confidant and close friend, Marjorie Putnam, also arrived to help with preparations. It was her porch companion and Thursday evening club mate, Lena, whose presence brought her to tears. To see Lena looking so healthy went a long way for Nana and it brought hope to us all.

When the fateful day came, I was whisked away from my husband by Collette and Nana. It was bad luck for him to see me before I walked down the aisle, they said. The ladies dressed me in a soft pink silk gown that fit my body like a glove. My pregnancy showed itself through the material, but quite honestly, I never felt more beautiful or feminine. My hair was brushed and parted down the middle before being twisted into a double knot that sat high on top of my head. The veil was placed in front of the knot, and its mesh covered my eyes and face.

Daniel and I exchanged wedding vows in front of nearly two hundred folks. So much for a simple wedding! All of the nurses and doctors who attended me, not to mention the patients who became my friends, were present for our very special wedding day. It was a glorious day indeed. The sun sat high in the sky, shining on all of us; the few leaves left hanging on the trees were emblazoned with color, and those that had already fallen, carpeted the ground with hues of red, orange, gold, and purples.

The food was splendid; Daniel admired the dishes so much that he sought the chef and asked about the ingredients and preparation. I knew Daniel's heart desired to be in a kitchen, not a prestigious architectural firm.

Our guests ate and drank until late into the night, but my husband had other ideas. He swept me away shortly after our vows and dinner, wishing to have me to himself, or so he said. I knew he wanted me to lay flat, take my rest, and produce a stunning heir.

"Let's stay here forever," Daniel said beside me in bed, rubbing my forearm with his fingers.

"I wish we could, but you have to finish your internship in order to graduate, Daniel."

"But I realize I'd rather be here, among family. It's better for you. I could open a restaurant with my father's help."

"I don't want to be indebted to your father, Daniel. I really don't. He is upset enough as it is." Daniel's father was the only noticeable figure absent from our wedding along with his wife, Quinn. He was not amused his son would marry someone with consumption and didn't wish to endorse our union.

"He'll have to get over that. I don't need his help then. I can work as a chef until we save enough money to have a place of our own, alongside a restaurant of our own."

"We could be right in town, Daniel, we could live above the restaurant to start. Then as we grow, the upstairs can be used for special events and parties."

"Yes, and we can have the house with the picket fence and wide open porch to enjoy during every season." The more we spoke, the more the idea took hold and became a plan.

"Make love to me, wife," Daniel commanded.

"Yes, sir," I answered, and our second wedding night was consummated.

The morning presented us with gifts galore. Nana's dining table was full to the brim with painstakingly wrapped packages begging to be opened. She sat with a pen and pad, taking note of who gave us what so that we might write our proper thank you notes. Daniel did the unwrapping, and I lay on the couch watching his every move. We received everything we would require for a house of our own. We also received ample gifts for the baby. Buntings and blankets, slippers, stuffed dolls, teething rings, and more elated us as we realized we really were to become parents. So far, my pregnancy was uneventful. I was blessed that I had no severe pains indicating a curvature of my spine. I felt better than I ever had in all my life. I promised to remember the first flutters of the baby's quickening, the thrill of the first kicks and the way my belly felt as the skin was pulled taught.

"We have a gift for you too, Mother," Daniel said.

"Now why would you go and do that?" she answered.

"We are planning on staying. We decided last night that we want to live here, with all of you."

"Yes, Nana, Daniel's heart isn't in architecture, he'd rather cook and have a restaurant of his own someday. We know it won't be easy at first; things will be tight for a while, but if we could stay in my old room?"

Nana brought her hands to her cheeks and jumped for joy; she hadn't exerted herself like this in some time.

"I am overjoyed. Yes, please do come home."

"We are here, I am only going back for our belongings and to wrap a few things up with the firm," Daniel said.

"Very well. We will get your room ready at once," she said through tears.

CHAPTER 24

❦

BLESSINGS

"How's my girl?" My faithful husband asked every day when he came home from work. He got a job with the catering company Nana used for our wedding reception and was very happy with his new occupation. He spent his days matting meatballs into perfect spherical shapes and making handmade raviolis and noodles. He enjoyed making sauces and anything savory. He was learning his way around a kitchen and I enjoyed sampling it all, as my appetite had grown along with my belly.

"I think I need to see Dr. Trudeau, my back is getting worse," I finally admitted when I could no longer stand the dull ache in my lumbar region. I kept my back pain to myself for a long time, Daniel massaged me every night to help ease me to sleep and I guided his expert hands to the lower regions that throbbed.

We made the appointment and Dr. Trudeau indicated I was slightly larger than he expected. He was unhappy with my progression and feared I would reactivate my disease and cause severe, irreversible damage to my vertebrae. The pain in my back is what gave him cause to be alarmed.

I wanted to be up and walking, because I felt certain it would help, but I was on strict bed rest and only allowed up to use the bathroom. Collette and Nana took turns guarding me and pampering me so that I wouldn't overdo it. They surprised me with an afternoon tea when I was in my seventh month. I was growing suspicious of all the whispering that was going on just out of earshot, but now I understood why. Friends and neighbors came to shower me with more gifts and well wishes for my family. We ate a yellow cake with thick chocolate frosting and talked about baby names.

That night I woke with sharp pains in my back so great that I couldn't stand it. We summoned the midwife at once and she prepared my birthing area right away.

Twelve hours later, my children were born. The intense pain I had experienced in the last twenty-four hours was from laboring, not vertebrae separating. Shortly after the midwife arrived, I felt the urge to push.

My son, Joseph Edward, and my daughter, Christine Collette Lyndon, who we called CeeCee, were born. My son weighed in at three pounds and two ounces and my daughter at three pounds five ounces. I was doubly blessed and thoroughly surprised. Although my husband wanted his son to take on his name, he understood why I had a change of heart and chose to name him Joe.

Once more, someone was looking down on me from the heavens. I thought a lot about my parents and siblings during this time, wishing they were here beside me to celebrate the birth.

When my husband walked into the birthing room, and saw me holding two bundles, one blue and one pink, he nearly fainted.

"Whoa, Nelly, I don't understand!" he exclaimed, bemused while he welcomed our children into the world with kisses and caresses. He grabbed the blue bundle and wept. He had a son. He had a healthy son. He held him by the light that seeped in through the window and studied his face. Then he came for the pink bundle, our daughter whom he cradled ever so gently. He studied her face and smiled from ear to ear.

"Are they both healthy, Gilly?" he asked the midwife.

"They are, Daniel. However, we must be extremely cautious because they are so small."

"How about my wife? Will she be okay?" he asked with a look of concern.

"Only time will tell, only time will tell," she repeated, before leaving us to nurture our children alone as a family for the first time.

Joseph Junior was colicky and fussy whenever he was apart from his sister. As soon as we laid them beside one another, swaddling them together, he calmed right down. Joseph was born with a mop of red hair like his father and CeeCee had blond fuzz with hints of strawberry.

Nana was certain all along that my child would be born healthy just as Collette's were. Nana was revived momentarily with her new grandchildren. She fussed over them like a mother hen, covering their toes, changing their diapers, and cuddling them endlessly.

One night Nana wept aloud at her fate. She wasn't allowed this time with her youngest son, and yet here she was with Daniel's children. Life had come full circle for her and she deemed it sacred and miraculous. We were happy we provided her with this joy.

Daniel and his mother often bottle fed the children at nighttime, they sat side by side and fed, then burped, the twins. It was a bonding time for a mother and her son, for he had finally come home.

The babies grew plump, but Nana took a turn for the worse. Nana was slipping away from us with each passing day. She grew even thinner and became exhausted with little to no effort. I, on the other hand, developed chronic back pain that kept me up at night. I was miserable and for the first time in my life, no amount of sheer will or optimism could take away my pain. Dr. Trudeau suggested casting me once more from shoulder to hip and I acquiesced. I was not on bed rest but was rendered immobile as a result of the thick, cumbersome, debilitating cast.

"If you maintain complete immobilization for a year, I think your spine will heal itself. Pott's disease, or spinal TB, is quite serious, as you know. You can suffer from destruction of the bone, or neurological complications. I realize a year is a long time, but I just don't think wearing a brace alone will keep you still enough."

"But, doctor, what about my babies?" I cried and cried. Sorrow filled my entire being, I felt sorry for myself and wished I wasn't cursed.

"Amy, I understand your frustration. Think of it this way, when your children are two years old and running around, you will be the one chasing them. Albeit, you'll be in a brace, but it will be you. Right now, it just can't be, but the blessing is they won't know the difference."

"But I will, I will know." For the first time in years, I let my heart open and spill out all the sorrow it contained. Losing my family, spending two years in a sanitarium alone, not obtaining my nursing degree and now this.

"I always tell you to be optimistic, and I know it's hard. I will give you one hour, and no more to brood, then I expect you will gather yourself and remember all your blessings."

He was right, as always. I gave myself permission to cry a little while longer. I was angry because I was not able to take care of my children and breastfeed them any longer. I couldn't cuddle them close to my chest and inhale their sweet scent.

I was enraged at TB, for it took lives and shattered dreams. I cried myself to the point of exhaustion. Then, as I always did in my past, I listed everything I had to be grateful for.

I was grateful to be alive. I was grateful to have a family who loved me and were willing to help raise my children while I was rendered immobile. I was grateful for my husband because he loved me with all his heart. Why he loved me I didn't know, but I know he did. I was grateful for the serenity I found in Saranac Lake, I was grateful for these magic mountains that took me in so long ago. I was grateful to call Collette my sister and to have had her by my side for so many years. My list continued. I felt restored and able to focus once more on what was important.

DANIEL

CHAPTER 25

❦

THE MAGIC MOUNTAINS

Mother passed away after my twins took their first steps. My wife was laying on the davenport with an afghan across her legs, biding her time until her brace was removed. Nana sat in her wing back chair with her needlework in a basket beside her. She was nearly done with her current project, a big sunflower pillow for the porch. The babies had been pulling themselves up on furniture for a few months and were edging along tables and chairs, taking steps as they went. CeeCee let go of the table and took two steps before tumbling. Not to be outdone, Joey did the same. My wife let out a whoop of excitement and clapped her hands for her children. It was the first of many of their milestones.

Amy charted this in the pink and blue baby books she kept beside the davenport at all times. The books held the babies' birth certificates with ink stampings of their feet, locks of hair, birth details, and milestones.

I thought my mother had nodded off as she often did, but when we clapped and cheered for the babies, she never moved a muscle. I knew something was terribly wrong, a few long strides and I was at her side, feeling for a pulse that didn't exist.

"Oh my God! Joe! Come quickly," I hollered for Joe, but he was out for his daily walk.

Always calm in the face of adversity, my wife asked for help rising. I went to her side and helped her into an upright position. She walked to Nana and covered her lap, held me tight, and said, "She's at peace, Daniel, with your brother and sister. It's okay."

Amy phoned Collette, who came at once with Will, and together they helped me make the necessary arrangements for Mother's funeral.

Enough flowers arrived to fill our house and line the stairs. The largest bouquet was from my father. He loved my mother to her last day. She was the woman who had his children, whom he cherished for over twenty years. She was his world at one time, but when the dreaded disease took hold of their family, he was unable to disguise his anxiety. His grief over losing his two children plagued him every day in much the same way the tuberculosis plagued Mother. It stifled him, isolated him, and drew him inward. I understood this. Now that I had children of my own, I couldn't begrudge my father for wanting to keep us safe and away from what he perceived as harmful.

He didn't come to the funeral, but he sent a letter to be buried with my mother. I am ashamed to say I broke his confidence and read the letter that professed his love and offered his sincerest apologies for not being by her side during her worst days. He was angry and upset enough with himself that I needed not judge him or lay him to blame for the years my mother spent alone, pining for him.

Saying goodbye to the matriarch of our family was unbearable, but in typical fashion, Amy made it okay for me somehow. My wife was a woman who took no moment for granted, she relished every second of every day that she was alive and felt certain my mother did, as well.

"She had a good life, Daniel, she tuned in to each moment and made them count. She kept a locket of all her children's hair and wore it every day. You were never far from her at all. She saw you married and met her grandchildren. She had a life that was full to the brim with love. What more could a woman ask for?"

"Good health," I answered.

"Daniel, I could ask for that too, but your mother taught me to live in the moment, each one is priceless. She never complained to me, not once, she accepted her fate; after all, it brought her to Joe and kept her close to Collette, and me."

"I know. It's just so hard saying goodbye. I missed having her in my life, I always thought about her but my father wouldn't allow me to visit. I wish I wrote more, in hindsight, I realize how much that would have meant."

"Don't beat yourself up, darling, you were a wonderful son. If anyone understood your precarious situation, it was your mother. She loved you more than life itself. She's at peace now. Let's not grieve for what we didn't have. Let's celebrate what we do have, what she had."

"Did I ever tell you about the time I tried to run away?" I laughed at the memory.

"No, you left that story out somehow."

"It was during those awkward teenage years. I was fourteen, all arms and legs, a real gangly fellow. I wanted to see my mother, I pined for her in the worst way, I just missed her, you know?"

Uh huh, go on."

"After dinner one night when Quinn was cleaning the dishes and my father was having a cigar, I approached him about visiting my mother. I told him I would use my own money, that I had enough saved from my allowance. He stopped the discussion at once and told me in no uncertain terms that visiting my mother was out of the question. I screamed at him, yelling that my mother and sisters were not lepers. I went on, though I knew he was mad enough to spit nails, and said I wouldn't come home all crippled with scabs covering my body. My father gave me a warning, he told me no son of his would be venturing to the Adirondacks and that I had better mind or else."

"What happened next?" I listened intently to this never before shared story.

"Well, I paid close attention to his work schedule and found out when he'd be gone for a long weekend. I hired a coach and bought a railway ticket to Saranac Lake."

"Oh, no, you didn't?"

"I surely did, only my father's meetings were canceled and he never went out of town. When the coach arrived, Father saw it approach before I had time to speak with the driver. When he learned I had defied him he sent me to the gallows."

"The gallows?"

"To the cellar actually, but to me it felt like the gallows. He used his belt and whipped me good; I have the scars to prove it. It was the only time he ever hit me, Amy, the only time."

"Goodness. Didn't he understand how vital it was for you to see your mother?"

"He did, he just couldn't get past his own grief and anxiety long enough to allow me to go. He was terrified, Amy. I imagine he still is."

"I don't get it. What is he so afraid of?"

"He's afraid of becoming like you, like my mother, and all the rest of the good, kind-hearted folks who have consumption. He used to wash his hands ferociously until they bled. His knuckles were always chapped and skin always dry. The man was so afraid of contagion that he let it rule his life, and mine."

"I'm sorry, Daniel, but part of me is glad your father stepped in. What if you did make that trip and caught your death from TB? Then I wouldn't have met you and had the pleasure of making you my husband. I wouldn't have two glorious children either."

"That's true. I suppose he kept me safe the best way he knew how."

Just then, Big Joe came in from his walk and sensed something was dreadfully wrong. He walked into the parlor where Amy sat comforting me and collapsed. The large man fell to the ground and lay in the fetal position. He cried until he was spent, and we let him be alone with my mother one last time. He held her hand and rocked back and forth on his haunches, swallowed up in memories shared with a remarkable woman.

We decided unanimously that my mother's funeral was to be a celebration of life. Marjorie Putnam and Dr. Kennedy traveled from Skaneateles to pay their respects to the woman who spearheaded the campaign in their town to stop tuberculosis dead in its tracks. My aunt and uncle, along with their children came to mourn, as did several of Mother's friends from Rochester whom she corresponded with regularly. My mother's best friend, Lena Thompson, spent the weekend at our house, she was no stranger to the disease, and had spent four years away from her own children while she took the cure. Many of these folks were here for our wedding and came back once more to honor the memory of my mother.

Not a family went unscathed or untouched by this disease and many held Mother in the highest regard for the way she handled herself both before she was diagnosed and after. My mother was stoic throughout her journey and that's how I would remember her.

At our celebration, Collette read my mother's favorite bible verse:

The LORD is my shepherd, I shall not be in want. He makes me lie down in green pastures, he leads me beside quiet waters, he restores my soul. He guides me in paths of righteousness for his name's sake. Even though I walk

through the valley of the shadow of death, I will fear
no evil, for you are with me; your rod and your staff,
they comfort me. You prepare a table before me in the
presence of my enemies. You anoint my head with oil;
my cup overflows. Surely goodness and love will follow
me all the days of my life, and I will dwell in the house
of the LORD forever.

– Psalm 23

My brothers, Big Joe, Dr. Trudeau, and I were the pallbearers along with a few other men. There wasn't a dry eye in the church when we eulogized her, but after laying her in the ground, the tears turned to laughter as everyone recalled my mother's tendency to take matters into her own hands. She led the charge to raise funds for tuberculosis in Skaneateles and in Saranac Lake, bringing in thousands of dollars with her Winter Festivals. The money was enough to build several new homes and cottages, as well as to pay for new doctors, nurses, and researchers for their hard work. My mother was a woman unlike any other. She didn't live in fear of her illness, she lived in spite of it.

The only other woman I would dare to place on a pedestal was my wife, and although she hated it, she would remain there for all my days. Amy took after my mother in many ways. She was never stingy with her laughter, she just chose to be happy and live a life that included loving deeply, smiling often, forgiving quickly, and having no regrets.

I learned this from my wife and applied it to my own life. I had dreams and wanted to see them to fruition.

I wanted to be a chef and manage my own restaurant. I learned the basics of making every sauce imaginable. I learned to make savory cream-based béchamels that used scalded milk as a base before being mixed with roux, spices, and then cheese. I made veloutes, a white stock-based sauce thickened with roux used in simple pasta dishes or over shrimp and fish. I learned to make a bordelaise sauce using red wine, shallots, bay leaf, garlic, pepper, and stock for numerous meat dishes and expanded upon this to make chasseur, a similar sauce rich with butter that was delightful over vegetables. I experimented making glazes and demi-glazes by using half brown and half white stock. This was best with fried steak and mushrooms. My wife enjoyed my hollandaise sauce the most, made from egg yolks, white vinegar, lemon, and garlic. She smothered asparagus spears or broccoli stalks with the creamy goodness that was designed for egg dishes. I added tarragon, chervil, and a pinch of nutmeg for poached eggs on toast and soon felt expert enough that I could move on to the next course.

I cooked mostly by trial and error. I watched my friend whose catering company served at my wedding, but I was a hands-on learner. I rolled up my sleeves in the kitchen and dug in to see what I liked together. My wife had a very discerning palette so I knew if she liked it, it was a winner.

Soon enough I had moved from sauces and meats, to side dishes, and then desserts. I was now ready to open my own restaurant. Mother left all her children a small sum of money. I used my funds to open "Christine's Restaurant" in downtown Saranac Lake that spring. I was taking a chance, but I had my wife's blessing and my mother looking over my shoulder. How could I fail?

Tuberculosis was the principle source of income in Saranac Lake. The town had tripled in size, boasting well over fifteen hundred inhabitants in 1895. My restaurant served the entire population. Many families with one or more members ill from consumption rented homes by the lake or in the mountains to take the cure. They dined on my cuisine regularly, as I was one of the first, and always crowded, kitchens in town. People were not used to dining out with their disease in public because they were shunned in other communities. Here, they could venture out in public and feel normal. Often folks asked for lunch to go, so I would pack them a lunch to take on a guided boat tour or wherever else they were headed. I catered their parties and weddings, or simply took the burden off a host who had too many mouths to feed and too little time to cook.

I would change my menu with the season. In the fall, we would dine on pumpkin raviolis, and squash soup alongside tender roasted chickens. In the winter, we could eat an abundance of root vegetables, meats, and cheeses to keep up our strength. Springtime would bring a wide variety of fruits and vegetables as this one had, to add to my main courses, which often included fresh bison or wild boar. Our lake trout was a popular meal and we began frying fish every Friday, serving it up with coleslaw and a potato mash.

Business thrived and very quickly my wife and I purchased our own home. We chose to live in the village proper, I could walk to work and my children could walk to school when they were older. With our departure, the cure cottage on River Street opened its doors to four more people who needed a place to stay while they healed.

Joe moved in with us. He was faring well even though he missed my mother something awful. He often spent time entertaining the children with his juggling acts and stories of his days in the circus. Many mornings, Joe would take the children out for breakfast so Amy and I could sleep in and have private time together. Her cast was a nuisance, but she was a trouper. She followed the doctor's orders to the finest detail and counted down the days until her cast was off.

During the moments we had alone, I would stand behind her while she sat in a chair. I would brush her long, thick, blond hair; it always sent tingles down her spine and made her feel alive. She described the sensation as erotic, and always wanted to be with me, but the cast got in the way so we loved each other in other ways such as this.

She cherished me and I felt it.

CHAPTER 26

❧

A CELEBRATION IS IN ORDER

The tumultuous year passed quickly and finally it was time for Amy's cumbersome cast to come off. I went with her to see Dr. Trudeau and held her hand as he sawed carefully through the plaster that had entombed her for so long. My wife's countenance was that of relief. Her back looked to be in excellent condition and the doctor was pleased. She would wear a brace that molded around her neck, collarbones, and back, but the difference was she could remove it. The brace would serve to hold her posture erect and keep her vertebrae in a straight column.

"This is a cause for celebration." I wanted to make love to my wife, it had been over a year since we had been together. We had put birth control measures in place and were free to carry on.

"What did you have in mind?" she asked with a devilish grin.

Joe took the children to the town's swan pond and fed the animals bits of stale bread. He walked them to the park and kept them out of our hair for half the day. When the children and Joe came home, they went sailing into their mama's arms and she was finally able to feel them against her skin once more.

"Thank God for Dr. Trudeau and his team, I can feel my babies again!" my wife said happily.

I prepared a chicken and dumpling soup to mark the occasion. It was a family favorite that everyone, including the children, gobbled up. My family was intact, my restaurant was thriving, and we had a roof over our heads.

I bought Amy a wooden collapsible easel to celebrate her release from the cast. The children gave her a new sketchpad and Joe bought her new watercolors and brushes. She was delighted with the gifts and spent time painting every day. Like my sister Collette, Amy had heightened artistic sensibilities, a skill she honed during her many years in solitude. However, she still felt the calling to nursing school and spoke of it often wistfully. She discussed this with Dr. Trudeau on more than one occasion that I overheard. The doctor had plans to open a school of nursing, now that the village was incorporated and he was the president, he could get to work on this structure.

EDWARD

CHAPTER 27

❦

EDWARD LIVINGSTON TRUDEAU

"Lottie, these mountains are magic indeed. Remember when Robert used to refer to them as the "ill-wild?" I said, unsticking my eyes and slugging down my morning cup of coffee.

"I do. He is a character that one, the whole Livingston clan, our dearest friends, I thank God for them every day. Lou will be here tonight to help us celebrate."

"Listen, Lottie, can you hear the leaves whispering in the wind?" I was feeling sentimental today for it was October fifth, my birthday. I had lived to see another year despite all the days that I thought to be my last.

My wife closed her eyes and listened for the soft symphony of leaves as the wind rolled through tree branches creating a sweeping, whispering hum. She rubbed her hand across my back and laid her head upon my shoulder as she often did.

"Just look around, won't you, Lottie? The census indicates we have over two thousand souls living here now. Everywhere you look, there are porches, why, we should name it, 'The Village of One Thousand Porches!'" I was mystified at how this once small hunters' paradise went from the untamed wild to a sophisticated town, home to esteemed writers, poets, artists, and even politicians.

"It's a sight to behold, dear," My wife remarked at how the most dreadful disease in history made our small town prosper, as tuberculosis was our primary income.

"So many taking the cure and thriving, not just living and getting by, but thriving, I dare say." I was enamored daily by the fact that people kept coming and building homes, taking the cure in our magical mountainside village.

"Like you," Lottie said.

"Yes, like me."

"They owe you a debt of gratitude, Edward. Without your heart and soul, none of this would be here." My wife gestured to the homes surrounding ours, as well as to the pristine mountains in the distance.

"Oh, I don't know about that, someone else would have connected the dots and figured out that mountain air was beneficial for TB."

"I doubt that, Edward. You did more than connect the dots. You buried yourself wholeheartedly into the study of the disease. You have lived it, researched it, treated it, and cured it for so many souls."

"They thought I was crazy when I immersed myself in this unbroken wilderness, a chest invalid wishing to live in the open air. Truly, I just wanted to live out my days hunting and fishing with the Livingston brothers. I never dreamed of this…" I gestured to all that was around me now.

"You should write an autobiography, darling. Tell the world your remarkable story." My wife was kneading my shoulders as she spoke.

"Whatever for? I am not a self-indulgent man. Only egomaniacs write autobiographies. Who wants to hear about my life?" I asked, eyes closed, enjoying the massage.

"Your son, Francis, for one. A memoir would serve the family well, not to mention the town."

I declined the idea, but that evening as we sat among our dearest lifelong friends, my wife brought out a particularly intriguing gift. It was too large to wrap, so was covered instead with a white cotton sheet. Lottie smirked, came toward me, and whipped the sheet off the mysterious item to reveal a typewriter.

"For your story, Edward." My wife kissed my cheek and my friends clapped me on the back, encouraging me to tell the story of the Sans.

"Where do I begin, Lottie? I am no writer; I am a scientist."

"Begin at the beginning," Lou chimed in, "how we ran wild as boys, and no one ever thought you'd make it as a doctor. I believe there was even a five hundred dollar wager on the table against your success," he said, wiping at his hawk-shaped nose with a hanky.

"Indeed there was, I had forgotten. I suppose I should leave a little something of myself in the world, if only for my son and medical research. I think I could write about the sanitarium, the magic mountains, and of the village that came to be." I didn't think I wanted to highlight the carefree days of my youth spent sailing and riding, although one of my life's highlights was the great Sappho Sailing Race I took part in.

"Yes, 'The Village of One Thousand Porches.' I like the sound of that," Lottie said, causing me to think back about our terrifying journey to the Adirondacks. Six of our seven horses gave out while trudging through the massive snowbanks and had to be cut loose far from our destination. It was our mare that pulled us through the heavy snow on our cutter. It's a miracle we survived the journey as well as our first winter at the isolated Paul Smith's Hotel.

Several evenings after my birthday celebration, I was staring intently at the great oil on canvas painting of my father in his Indian hunting regalia, forcing me to reminisce. I didn't grow up with the man who was my father but rather with my mother in France. My parents separated and divorced, splitting the children between them. My father took my sister with him to New York, and my mother took my brother and me with her. My father was a doctor and huntsman like me, so I supposed my love for medicine and hunting was in the blood. I didn't, however, spend two years of my life living among the Osage Indians as he did to learn their culture and language. I hunted for sport, initially but later for research specimens. Thankfully, Lottie allowed me to contain my catches in our basement so that I could study them thoroughly. A lesser woman would have grown weary of the care and keeping of so many wild animals, but not my Lottie. I missed having the hounds about me now; old Bunnie was the rarest of hounds, able to stick to one rabbit's track without getting derailed.

I sat at my typewriter and clicked away at the keys, starting with my birth and upbringing in France alongside my brother Francis, my most faithful companion. When he was diagnosed with tuberculosis, I cared for him single handedly. His confinement and demise elicited an empathy from me that later prompted me to attend medical school. This was a most painful memory, but necessary to write about because this experience helped shape the man I would become.

I wrote every detail of my wedding to my wonderful wife, Lottie, who always met life's struggles head on. A remarkable woman, my Lottie; where I was impulsive she was practical, she balanced me and supported me. She was a true, life partner.

I reminisced about my four children, three of whom have passed away before me. I ruminated and allowed the sorrow to take me to a grievous place for a moment when remembering my daughter Chatte who looked so much like her mother. Then I thought of Ned and Henry as infants. Each of their births brought forth hope, and with each of their passing, they took a part of my soul.

A parent should never know the pain of burying a child, and I have buried three. Lottie was stoic when I faltered and insisted on focusing on the positive. Francis, our youngest child, became our pride and joy. Today he is a healthy and robust lad who will carry on the family name and legacy.

I scribbled notes, formed outlines and thought of my life's turbulent moments, such as the cold abscess that was found in my teen years, a predictor for tuberculosis. If I had only been diagnosed, then I would have led a healthier life for certain. Or the swollen lymph glands, another predictor that was misdiagnosed as scrofula, which I treated with painted iodine and a breakfast tonic. One more opportunity for an early diagnosis and better outcome was missed while on my honeymoon in Europe. Finally, as a medical doctor working at The Strangers Hospital, a coworker commented over my rundown condition. My once slender, athletic build had collapsed into a scrawny, slumped frame that I attributed to long hours and little rest. My endurance waned as well, prompting the appointment that changed my life. I went to see a Dr. Janeway, who was an expert diagnostician; my examination revealed that the upper three quarters of my left lung had active TB. Consumption was synonymous with death. I had seen it with my own brother and many others. I was doomed and forlorn and angry with myself for missing the symptoms. The delivery of the diagnosis made on that day has never left my mind and has served me well in my professional practice. I learned in that precise moment to be merciful when telling a patient they are positive for tuberculosis.

After my diagnosis, my gradual demise ensued. I was instructed to ride horses daily and to keep up a rigorous exercise regimen, but I lost weight and was unable to reduce my fever. My strength lessened, and I was forced to give up work. Feeling I had little time left to live, I chose to go to the Adirondack Mountains, a place that had always brought me peace and serenity. I left my wife, and then, two children, behind under the guardianship of my colleague, Dr. Walton. My good friend Lou Livingston took me through Plattsburgh to the mountains. I was so ill and frail that we had to stay in Plattsburgh for two nights so that I might get some rest to continue with our journey. My friend conjured a very old-fashioned horse and buggy, fitting it with a mattress and several fluffy pillows so that I could lay down and ride more comfortably for the rest of the arduous journey. By the time we reached the Paul Smith Hotel, I was so feverish that the proprietor of the hotel, a large specimen of a man with great strength, had to scoop me up and carry me up a set of stairs to my room. The guides and patrons of the Hotel came up to see me and bring me cheer. Like me, they were doubtful I would make it through the night. Alas, when I woke, my fever had broken. Mrs. Smith provided me with a hearty breakfast of eggs, bacon, mutton, and fruit, and I was able to eat it all. As the days passed, I regained my appetite and felt remarkably better than I had in some time. I went hunting with the guides-men of the mountains; we hunted rabbits, the elusive red fox, and deer. I was an excellent shot for one so feeble and weak. When compared to the sturdy men around me, my aim took down far more birds than theirs and I brought in more rabbits than all the men combined. The men took me fishing and boating as well; they did the rowing while I lay in the vessel, feeling the steady progress of the boat as it glided through the water.

When I recount the summer spent in the mountains and how rejuvenating it was, it's no wonder that I decided to stay on for the winter. Many claimed I was suicidal. Surviving a harsh winter in the mountains, in a primitive facility, with no running water, was desperate. Luckily, I spent it alongside the Smith family most uneventfully. We spent many evening sitting together around the fire, telling stories, playing cards, or what have you. I even learned the Morse alphabet that winter.

The following year I brought my family to winter with me. We found a decent place to live in the town of Saranac Lake. The home was sixteen square feet and came to us unfurnished. Mrs. Smith, who was a most admirable and generous lady, provided us with all the comforts of a home including pots and pans as well as beds and quilts. The winters were hardly bearable; we had no coal, and when the thermometer dipped below zero, we woke up to a layer of ice across our furnishings. Our first year in Saranac Lake, we lost our son to an illness that sent him into convulsions and then his death two days later.

Following my son's death, my exacerbations waned, my fevers were controlled, and I began to wonder about opening a health resort in this remote part of the mountains. I met Doctor Loomis while at Paul Smith's, he had a practice in New York and agreed to send patients to Saranac Lake for a trial period such as my own. With more invalids in the mountains for treatment, the place gradually grew from the once rough hillside covered in scant grass and boulders to the place we now called home.

I stopped my note taking and tabulations for a moment and stood to pace. I picked up my gold watch, which lay on the table before me and turned it over to read the inscription. "E. L. Trudeau, from the Saranac Boys." The guides I had come to rely on wanted me to have a sufficient timepiece instead of the old tin one I used so that I could practice medicine once more.

The men I met while staying at Paul Smith's Hotel had become my most faithful companions and friends. It is hard to describe the relationships we developed over the years, but I count myself lucky to have maintained these friendships for the course of my life. In fact, it was these same men, and a few others, who pooled their money and purchased the sixteen acres of land where my sanitarium sits. When they presented me with the deed, we each grew embarrassed from the sentiment.

The acreage was uninhabited and had rocks and boulders that jutted five feet or more out of the ground. We had no running water and were indeed a very primitive facility. Our house with its attached laboratory, and our humble Little Red, the pioneer cottage, was just the beginning. I remember not knowing what I had gotten myself into, for I didn't know how to run a health resort, nor did I know how to build cottages. But I knew I wanted to utilize a cottage plan in order to segregate the patients rather than aggregate them as they did in the hospitals. I hired a man by the name of M. J. Norton to run the facility, his wife and two daughters were hired as well, and they did the cooking and cleaning.

I missed having a church nearby to worship, so we started a subscription list for a small log chapel. Calling on old friends for donations for the church was just the beginning of begging my friends for money. The church, St. John's in the Wilderness, was constructed with logs donated by Paul Smith, not just any logs but white pine logs of exceptional size and quality. Stained glass windows were donated along with a brass book rest, linen, and an organ. We even had a bishop's chair donated and any priest was welcome to the pulpit to give a sermon on any occasion.

Our first two patients spent their cure time in Little Red, as primitive as she was, she was barely outfitted, and when the ladies arrived from their two-day journey, they were at death's door.

All this writing and remembering was exhausting. I sipped at my tea and closed my eyes once more, drifting back in the recesses of my mind to the fires. The fires took so much from me, but taught me a thing or two as well.

The temperatures were below zero degrees outdoors the fateful night of the fire. The bunnies we housed would stay warm huddling together in their hutch, but if I didn't make an arrangement to keep my guinea pigs warm they wouldn't survive the night. I decided to run the heater from my laboratory all night for the pigs and at three a.m. we smelled the smoke. The heater caught fire and burned down the entire lab, all my medical equipment, including my one and only microscope and slides, as well as part of my home. It was a devastating moment, for my career's research burned to the ground.

The fire occurred precisely when I was immersed in the study of Koch's papers, The Etiology of Tuberculosis. I found his painstaking experimentation to be solid. Koch concluded that "germs" caused the widespread disease that caused TB. Most researchers rejected his theories, although I held them in high esteem. During this time, I also studied alongside a Dr. Prudenn in New York who was known for his prowess in pathology. It took some time to get him to warm to me, but when he did, he taught me the principals of bacteriology and how then to isolate and stain tubercle bacillus. After years of conferring with him, gaining his expertise and knowledge, I was able to cultivate the tubercle bacillus. I was the first researcher in the country to do so, and now the slides I had so thoroughly and painstakingly created were destroyed by fire.

Imagine my delight when I was presented then with an early Christmas gift from Dr. Prudenn and his team of researchers. It was a new microscope, a fine instrument with all the necessary objectives. The letter read:

"My Dear Dr. Trudeau:

We men at the laboratory want to make you a Christmas present, and we are so eager in wanting to that we cannot wait till the proper time.

I don't think we have decided whether we want to do this most because we appreciate the good work you are always doing, in our line and others, or because you have had more pluck than anybody we know or because you have been so often helpful to us and made us always glad to have you here, or because—well the fact is, old fellow, we all like you and want you to know it and so here we are in a row, bestowing our early Christmas greeting."

I keep this letter folded in a tin box alongside my other most valuable letters.

The afternoon following the fire I was visited by our dear friends, the Coopers, who offered to build me a new laboratory made from stone and steel, providing I planned it. Plan it I did and within the year we had a newly constructed laboratory for my research within a fireproof brick building so that I could continue my studies utilizing my new microscope. Once I had pure cultures, I tried killing the germ with the injection of carbolic acid, creosite, and other substances. But the tubercle bacillus could not be destroyed. Because it was a germ, I began to wonder how it gained access to the body, and then further, I wondered how it was that a person's environment could alter the germ's state.

1. Edward Livingston Trudeau, *An Autobiography*, (Philadelphia and New York, Lea & Febiger, 1915), 181.

I began experimenting with rabbits, inoculating three lots. The first lot, Lot 1, was injected with pure cultures and released into the best possible surroundings; light, open air, and food were abundant. The second lot, Lot 2, was also inoculated but these were put in deplorable conditions, a dank basement, little circulating air, and minimal food sources. The third lot, Lot 3, was put under similar bad conditions without being inoculated.

My findings were astounding. From Lot 1: Of all the rabbits that were able to run in the open air, all but one survived. From Lot 2: All the rabbits but one died from the disease and their organs showed extensive TB. Finally, Lot 3's rabbits were killed and dissected and were found to have no TB disease. Thus, bad surroundings in and of themselves could not be responsible for the disease. Once the germs gained access to the body, the environment in which the host lived had a profound effect on the course of the disease.

I put my findings in a paper and was scheduled to speak in Baltimore in front of an audience of medical professionals. Imagine my humiliation, then when I felt hot and dizzy and fainted on the spot, unable to read from my paper. Instead, I listened from a horizontal position while a colleague with a booming voice read off my findings!

I continued my research and tried repeatedly to find a germicide that would kill TB. I had no luck whatsoever in finding a treatment or a product that would produce a real immunity to TB. Years passed by and I spent more time in bed with exacerbations of my own. I took the cure as did my patients at the Sans, my mind often unable to still itself while I rested.

During these years, the illustrious Robert Louis Stevenson came to Saranac Lake. It was during his time here that he penned some of his most famous works. Mr. Stevenson and I had numerous interesting and often heated discussions in his sitting room. While I found him to be an idealist of the highest order, I still quite enjoyed his company. When he left Saranac Lake, he sent me a gift of his works; it was a bound set, written in his own hand. He dedicated *Dr. Jekyll and Mr. Hyde* to my dog, Nig, and *Treasure Island* to my son Ned. He dedicated three other works to my family as well, but these two were my favorites.

During this time, we were blessed with a new baby, whom we baptized and named Francis. He was a godsend, as our strong, athletic daughter, Chatte, who was studying in New York, fell ill. We brought Chatte home to live out her days with us; she had the type of TB that progressed rapidly much like that of my brother. I knew her days were numbered and so did she. I took care of my daughter in her illness as well as the patients residing in cottages at the Sans. I caught a horrible case of whooping cough from Francis, and suffered tremendously as a result. Never was there a time when our friends showed their true colors more. One dear friend took over the infirmary at the Sanitarium during this trial, and my friend Dr. Baldwin from New York presented himself in Saranac Lake to help where he could.

When Chatte died, my friends from the laboratory along with Paul Smith, his wife, and their sons, attended the funeral at the log cabin church, St. Johns in the Wilderness. Many friends, patients, and family members stood by our side as we suffered tremendous sadness. They encouraged us along and helped us throw ourselves back into our productive lives at the Sanitarium. Heartbreak aside, we constructed nine new cottages from 1887–1889 and also built an open-air pavilion for recreational activities. A billiards table was donated and many folk took kindly to the addition.

We constructed an infirmary cottage for those who were extremely ill, a place where they could be cared for around the clock. We also established a home for a resident physician during this time. A fund was established by anonymous donors that allowed us to construct a new laboratory near the infirmary as well as an illustrious library wing.

I stopped my writing for a moment and wondered where to take it from here. I had yet to discuss the passing of my son Ned, and didn't wish to now, for it was too painful. Not any less painful than the passing of Chatte, it's just that the wound was still too fresh. I fear my wife and I will never recover from our sorrow.

"Lottie, have a read will you? I don't want to get too detailed with my pen, for people will surely get bored by my ramblings," I said to my wife, after one long afternoon spent typing and reminiscing.

"Certainly, darling, anything for you," she responded with enthusiasm as always.

She spent the next few days poring over my notes and writings, correcting dates where necessary and tearing up at the memory of losing Chatte and Ned.

"It's a beautiful testament to your work," she finally said one afternoon as she lay down the last piece of paper. "The only thing that I see missing is you. Yes, you detail your youth and our courtship, followed by your training in medical school and life at the Sans. However, you don't detail yourself, dear."

"Well, how am I to do that?"

"I will do it for you if you wish. I want Francis and anyone else who reads your autobiography to know what a handsome and kind man you are. I want them to see your courage and strength in the face of so much adversity. You hardly detail your own ills, why the abscess on your kidney has had you in pain and anguish for years. You can hardly sleep for more than an hour or so at a time as a result."

"But, dear, I am far from handsome, why look at my high forehead and beak of a nose. Nor am I strong and courageous. I am simply an optimist, a weakling optimist, but an optimist." I admitted I was in sad shape, and hated that my disease and now kidney condition kept me feverish and bedridden more often than not these days. I had to rely on so many people to do the work that I had undertaken from the start.

"Yes, you are the ultimate optimist, it's what has kept you living all these years, it's what you preach to your patients. But, darling, you are the most courageous and strong-willed person I know. You have overcome your own exacerbations and continued along to help others who suffer. You have brought hope to hundreds, husband. You have brought hope and light to people who otherwise wouldn't have had it. You saved lives. When you started your Free Bed Fund, you opened the doors to people of little means so they had a chance to heal. Look at Lena; if not for the funds you procured she would not have had a bed. After a few years here, her symptoms arrested, and she was able to go home to her family. You single handedly changed her life for the better. You researched and diligently pressed forward with experiments to learn about this disease in a way no other man has. You are a hero, my husband. A real hero."

"Oh for heaven's sake, bite your tongue. I am just a simple man."

"It's true, it is why the Sans is nicknamed 'Hope on the Hill.' Look at you now, you are burning up with fever, yet you dismiss it. Instead you replace it with talk about a nursing program and a program that would allow other doctors to come to the Sans and learn from you. You had a vision and look at it now. Up from the crab grass to all these lives saved and impacted."

"You're embarrassing me, Lottie, stop at once."

"Never you mind about being embarrassed, I am allowed to give praise where I see fit. I am not alone, I know for a fact Christine felt the same way, God rest her soul. Not to mention how you helped Collette get into nursing school, and Amy, she was your first extra pulmonary patient and you cared for her so diligently."

"I suppose you could call me Cupid. Look at the couples that formed here. I think my favorite was Big Joe and Christine; they were meant to be together."

"As were Daniel and Amy. A grand family with children of their own now."

"It has been a remarkable journey, Lottie, that much I will admit. All the people I have met along the way, healthy or not, have shaped me and thus, the Sans into what it is today."

"That's true, we must give credit where credit is due. But, Edward, it was you who went knocking on doors to raise funds and you whose insight made it happen."

"Don't remind me of all the doors I knocked upon begging for money, it still rattles me. I was so nervous and uncomfortable asking for funds."

"But you did, and look what the monies brought about."

"Yes, and I hope the Sans will continue to grow as we have a proper endowment fund now, being handled by Stephen Baker at the Bank of the Manhattan Company. Thankfully, he is a trustee as well."

"The Sanitarium's trustees, your friends, Edward, everyone is in awe of you; most of all me."

"At the end of the day, Lottie, when I close my eyes to drift into a slumber I have faith. Faith that one day, early detection will be the predominant treatment for this disease. I have faith in people, my self-sacrificing friends and colleagues, the doctors, nurses, administrators, and scientists all who are making a difference. But mostly, my dear, I have faith in you. You are the best wife a man could have. Without you by my side, picking me up when I was down, I would not have been inspired and encouraged to overcome so many obstacles, or to set so many lofty goals."

My wife came to me then, sweetly pressing her lips to mine, unafraid of becoming ill, loving me for who and what I am. A man with a dreadful disease known as TB.

PHOTOS FROM THE SANS

Dr. Edward Livingston Trudeau
Photo courtesy of the Adirondack Collection, Saranac Lake Free Library

Dr. Trudeau in his lab

Paul Smith's Hotel, circa 1880
Photo courtesy of the Adirondack Collection, Saranac Lake Free Library

Female patients curing
Photo courtesy of the Adirondack Collection, Saranac Lake Free Library

Male patients curing
Photo courtesy of the Adirondack Collection, Saranac Lake Free Library

"Little Red" Cottage
Photo courtesy of the Adirondack Collection, Saranac Lake Free Library

Adirondack Cottage Sanitarium
Photo courtesy of the Adirondack Collection, Saranac Lake Free Library

Adirondack Cottage Sanitarium
Photo from cardcow.com

ABOUT THE AUTHOR

Julie Dewey is a novelist who is inspired by history. In her dreams, she lives in the 19th century but in reality she resides with her family in Central New York, America's snow capital.

Julie is passionate about jewelry design and gemstones, she loves anything and everything creative. If she isn't writing, she can be found decorating, knitting, decoupaging, stamping, scrapping, working with metal, shopping, or napping.

Visit Julie at www.juliedewey.com for a book group guide.

BOOK GROUP QUESTIONS

✦

1. How did the first person account of each character help you to see into each individual's story? If written from only one character's perspective, whose voice would you choose and why?

2. On the surface, the lives of the patients who inhabit the Sans are very different, but in what ways are they similar?

3. When Christine found out she was pregnant, did you think that should have altered her course of care for Collette in order to protect the health of her unborn child?

4. When little Joe was born, did you think it was right or wrong of Christine to stay on at the Sans? Do you think Collette felt guilty for this situation?

5. What do you find the most remarkable about this story?

6. How did Collette and Amy dare to dream from their cure chairs? In what way does having a positive attitude influence their stories?

7. Lena, a mother of three, was faced with a very difficult choice. What would you have done in her situation?

8. Do you believe in love at first sight as in the case of Amy and Daniel?

9. In theory, people who took the cure had heightened artistic and philosophical sensitivities. Why do you think this is?

10. Is there a happy ending for any of the folks from Saranac Lake?

11. If you lived in Saranac Lake, would you have wanted people infected with plague to come live in your town? What did you think about the town's hospitality toward the infected?

12. Describe Edward Trudeau in one word.

13. Did you feel inspired after reading this book? If so, in what way?

ABOUT THE BOOK

❦

What prompted you to write a book about TB sanitariums?

My mother had the idea to write about the TB sanitariums, which were widely used in the late 1800s through the mid-1900s. She always suspected that her own mother, Grace, had a touch of TB as scar tissue showed up in her later years on a series of x-rays.

While writing and researching for this book, we found out my great grandmother, Lena, Grace's mother, was actually in a TB sanitarium for several years, quite possibly in the Adirondack's. This intrigued me further and compelled me to wonder if, in fact, my grandmother, Grace had TB that went undetected.

What type of research did you do for the book?

I studied my own family history with the help of my aunts and uncle, who so graciously took time from their lives to write out their accounts of Lena and Grace. I also read many books and detailed accounts of what it was like to be in a sanitarium from patients themselves, or their children. My favorite book, however, was Edward Livingston Trudeau's autobiography. He was such an incredible human being, and thankfully, he opened the Sans and saved thousands of lives. The Edward Livingston Trudeau museum in Saranac Lake is on my must-see list.

What surprised you the most when you were doing your research?

While doing my research it surprised me just how many people were afflicted with TB and how many lives were lost. I was also surprised at how romanticized the disease was, yet it affected everyone, and was purely awful. Finally, not to have any cure while suffering seems impossible to understand for those of us living in today's world. To deem 'open air' as a cure was remarkable in and of itself.

The other thing that surprised me was the generosity and goodwill of Trudeau's friends. All the guides-men who donated time and money to the Sans, as well as the bankers and businessman who became trustees were altruistic and trusting of Edward and his vision.

Discuss your personal association to the topic.

I have chronic asthma, which makes it very difficult to breathe on occasion, even with proper medication. I do not have TB, but because it can be, and is most often, associated with the lungs, I can relate, somewhat, to what these folks endured. I have suffered attacks so brutal that I became terrified for my life, I can only imagine the patients at the Sans felt this way on many occasions. Yet they had to maintain positive attitudes and hope in order to get well again.

What was it like to write from the typical TB patient's point of view?

It is tricky to write from a patient's point of view, not being one. I tried to conjure several different personality types from numerous backgrounds and bring them together in a place and time when they would not normally have associated. I particularly liked writing about the gracious folks who were friends of, or family members, of the patients; they often were even more remarkable in their generosity. People like the Smith family were generous, kind, and helpful in numerous ways.

What surprises you the most about your characters?

I love that all the characters in the book had a survival mentality. Regardless of their station in life, they all met their conditions head on and made the most of their circumstances. I admire them and the way they handled themselves so gracefully, having hope and faith that better days were ahead.

NOTES

❧

NOTES

NOTES

❦

NOTES

CPSIA information can be obtained at www.ICGtesting.com
Printed in the USA
BVOW05s1801110916

461491BV00001B/1/P